THE SPIRITUAL RETREAT

Iʿtikāf

THE PHILOSOPHY, SPIRITUAL MYSTERIES, AND PRACTICAL RULINGS

Compiled and Translated by Saleem Bhimji
Edited by Arifa Hudda

Iʿtikāf: The Spiritual Retreat

The Philosophy, Spiritual Mysteries, and Practical Rulings

Compiled and Translated by Saleem Bhimji

Edited by Arifa Hudda

ISBN: 978-1-927930-50-2

Published by Islamic Publishing House · www.iph.ca · iph@iph.ca

Cover Design and Text Layout by Saleem Bhimji

The photo on the cover of this book was taken by Saleem Bhimji and features the meḥrāb (prayer niche) of the Az-Zahraa Islamic Centre in Richmond, British Columbia, Canada (www.az-zahraa.org)

Table of Contents

In the Name of Allah,

the All-Compassionate,

the All-Merciful

Dedication

This work is dedicated in the memory of the following dearly departed individuals. Please take a moment to recite Sūrah al-Fātiḥa one time, followed by Sūrah al-Ikhlāṣ three times for their reward, and the reward of all the martyrs, scholars, and believers who left this world on the path of true faith.

Marḥūma Ḥājjah Ashraf Devji

Marḥūm Murtaza Akberali Walji

Transliteration Table

The method of transliteration of Islamic terminology from the Arabic language has been carried out according to the standard transliteration table mentioned below.

ء	ʾ	ض	ḍ
ا	a	ط	ṭ
ب	b	ظ	ẓ
ت	t	ع	ʿ
ث	th	غ	gh
ج	j	ف	f
ح	ḥ	ق	q
خ	kh	ك	k
د	d	ل	l
ذ	dh	م	m
ر	r	ن	n
ز	z	و	w
س	s	ي	y
ش	sh	ه	h
ص	ṣ		

Long Vowels		Short Vowels	
ا	ā	ـَ	a
و	ū	ـُ	u
ي	ī	ـِ	i

Symbols Used in this Book

عزّ وجلّ

Free from Imperfections and Exalted is He - Used for Allāh عزّ وجلّ

صلى الله عليه وآله

Prayers of Allah be upon him and his Family - Used for Prophet Muḥammad صلى الله عليه وآله

عجل الله تعالى فرجه الشريف

May Allah hasten his noble advent – Used for Imam al-Mahdī عجل الله تعالى فرجه الشريف

عليه السلام

Peace be upon him - Used for notable male personalities

عليها السلام

Peace be upon her - Used for notable female personalities

عليهم السلام

Peace be upon them - Used for three or more notable personalities

قدس سره الشريف

May their spirit be sanctified - Used for deceased scholars

Translator's Introduction

Our journey to publish a comprehensive work on something as profound and impacting as *Iʿtikāf* began over 15 years ago when we were blessed by Allah ﷻ to translate and publish an article entitled: *Iʿtikāf: The Spiritual Retreat.*[1] This article continues to be hosted on numerous websites and has been used by countless individuals around the world in preparation for their *iʿtikāf* and has even been referenced in an Academic Journal, *Jurnal Kajian Wilayah - Journal for Area Studies* in a piece entitled: "The Life of Muslim Indonesian Students in Germany: Challenges and Opportunities" by Gilang Maulana Majid.[2]

As we embark on yet another season of worship during the months of Rajab, Shaʿbān, and the blessed month of Ramaḍān, those wishing to engage in the highly meritorious act of *iʿtikāf* will once again be searching for authentic guidance - from both the Philosophical, and Jurisprudential aspects - on how to carry out this unique act of worship in

---

[1] This can be found on: www.al-islam.org/articles/itikaf-spiritual-retreat-saleem-bhimji - Last accessed on March 22, 2023.

[2] https://jkw.psdr.lipi.go.id/index.php/jkw/article/view/778 - Last accessed on February 3, 2024.

which they will seclude themselves in a masjid in devotion to Allah ﷻ.

For this reason, we decided to revisit this topic, and present this comprehensive book which looks at *iʿtikāf* in three phases:

1. The first section is a thorough introduction to *iʿtikāf* and focuses on establishing the basis for what is to come in the remainder of this book. It also contains spiritual guidance from four contemporary senior scholars of Islam.
2. The second section is a translation of an in-depth research piece concerning *iʿtikāf* - the spiritual retreat[3] which looks at this unique act of worship from multiple Philosophical and Spiritual angles.
3. The final section of this book contains guidelines on *iʿtikāf* based on the most recently published rulings of Āyatullāh Sayyid ʿAlī al-Ḥusaynī al-Sīstānī, may Allah protect and preserve him and all the other righteous scholars, taken from his multi-volume Islamic Laws manual written in Farsi.

We hope and pray that this multi-faceted study of *iʿtikāf* results in a transformation in those seeking spiritual openings as they dedicate themselves to Allah ﷻ in a masjid during the most important days and nights of the Islamic calendar.

---

[3] Throughout this book, we will interchangeably use the terms *iʿtikāf* and 'spiritual retreat' as a translation of *iʿtikāf*.

What is Iʿtikāf?

Iʿtikāf is one of the most unique acts of devotion to Allah ﷻ found within the teachings of Islam. What is deemed as a "spiritual retreat" entails that a believer - a man or woman - secludes oneself in the House of Allah ﷻ - a proper, religiously-defined masjid - for a set period of time.

During the duration of *iʿtikāf*, individuals engage in worship, contemplation, and reflection on the self - all in an attempt to get spiritually closer to Allah ﷻ, seeking to improve themselves, and become better human beings. This act - which is done for a minimum of a three-day period - is a unique form of worship in Islam, as we will explore in this introduction, and then in greater depth later on in this book.

In his book, *Why Does God Command Me?*, Shaykh ʿAlī Riḍā Panāhiyān states: "The word *iʿtikāf* in Arabic means staying in one place. *Iʿtikāf* in religious terminology means staying in the masjid for at least three days. During this stay, one should not leave the masjid unless necessary, and he/she must fast during the days. *Iʿtikāf* is not a worship act done by force. Rather, it is a voluntary worship act with the aim of getting closer to God..."[4]

When a believer makes an intention to engage in the spiritual retreat, they do so for a minimum of three days - the first two days are their own prerogative, however once they have intended to devote themselves to Allah ﷻ, then the third day becomes an obligation *(wājib)* to complete. In essence, Allah ﷻ has now welcomed you as His guest in His House,

---

[4] Panāhiyān, ʿAlī Riḍā, *Why Does God Command Me?*, Pg. 8.

the masjid, and what an amazing host He is and what an amazing venue that He accommodates His visitors in!

In normal circumstances, it is highly undesirable *(makrūḥ)* to sleep in the masjid - after all, it is not a hotel! However, during *iʿtikāf*, it becomes an obligation to spend the entire time in the House of Allah ﷻ - in other words, Allah ﷻ WANTS us to be in His Proximity and spend time in His House.

Later on in the same book, Shaykh Panāhiyān states: "It is abominable to stay in the masjid overnight unless it is for *iʿtikāf*. You use this opportunity to experience sleeping in the masjid. This brings about an awakening. It is as if masjids have some hidden parts, which you are able to discover when you stay in them for a period. You stay so that when others go, you may sit waiting for the masjid to show its internal reality to you."[5]

Another unique aspect of *iʿtikāf* is that although it is done in a group setting - that is tens, hundreds, or even thousands of like-minded Muslim men and women are all devoting themselves to Allah ﷻ in the same building, engaging in the same activities, and breathing the same air - however, it is very much a personal journey and experience.

Although you are surrounded by others, taking in the environment with all of your senses, at the same time, you are alone with the One.

Further in his review, Shaykh Panāhiyān states: "At the same time that you are with the crowds, try to not lose your

---

[5] *Why Does God Command Me? Chapter on: What Does God Expect From Me?*, Pg. 15.

solitude either. We are unable to understand that the world is in God's presence, and we are unable to feel His presence. Therefore, it is good if we go to the masjid and try to feel God's presence since His presence is more tangible in the masjid. At least one time, feel His presence here a little deeper than all other times and places. After leaving the masjid, we will still feel we are in His presence for a while."[6]

The Beauty of Iʿtikāf

Iʿtikāf is not just a spiritual sojourn - it is a break from the temporal world and all of its allure - the hectic work schedules, or the pressures of school, and the mindless scrolling on social media. It is to detach from everything: family, friends, society, and the world around us; then attach oneself to the only thing that truly matters - Allah ﷻ.

May Allah ﷻ enable those who have never taken the steps to partake in *iʿtikāf* the Divine blessings *(tawfīq)* to engage in this spiritual sojourn at least once in their lifetime and may He accept their efforts. May Allah ﷻ keep the love of *iʿtikāf* alive in the hearts of all believers and give them the spiritual longing to devote themselves to Him on a yearly basis. May we live to see the day when we can perform *iʿtikāf* in the sacred Shrines of the Ahlul Bayt ﷺ, alongside our living and awaited saviour, Imam al-Mahdī عجل الله تعالى فرجه الشريف.

[6] *Why Does God Command Me? Chapter on: What Does God Expect From Me?*, Pg. 16.

Iʿtikāf in the Words of the Scholars[7]

What follows in this section is the spiritual guidance from four contemporary *marājiʿ taqlīd* in which they offer their advice to believers with respect to this unique act of worship known as *iʿtikāf.*

Taking in the words of wisdom from these great scholars of Islam and doing our best to implement the guidance which undoubtably, they themselves have practiced before they have encouraged us to do so - will help us go a long way on the path of refinement of the soul and attaining spiritual proximity to Allah ﷻ.

Imprison the Passions of the Soul[8]

---

[7] Extracted from an article on www.hawzah.net - Last accessed on March 23, 2023 (with minor edits).

[8] This piece was written by Āyatullāh Ḥusayn Waḥīd Khorāsānī who was born in 1921 in Nishāpūr, Mashad in Iran.

Having finished his introductory Islamic studies, he moved to the second stage, known as *sutūḥ,* and continued to the final stage known as *baʿth al-khārij.* At the age of 27, he migrated to Najaf al-Ashraf in Iraq to complete his studies and attended the lectures of the late Āyatullāh Mīrzā ʿAbdul Hādī Shīrāzī ؒ, and late Āyatullāh Muḥsin al-Ḥakīm ؒ, with his main teacher being the late Āyatullāh Abūl Qāsim al-Khuʾī ؒ.

In 1958, after teaching the secondary stage of Islamic Studies, Āyatullāh Waḥīd Khorasānī began teaching *Fiqh* and *Uṣūl* at the highest stage in Najaf, a position which he carried out for over twelve years. In 1936, he returned to Iran, took up residence in

What is *iʿtikāf?* Simply put, *iʿtikāf* is self-restraint.

We must wake up from the sleep of spiritual negligence *(ghaflah),* thus the reality of *iʿtikāf* is that it is a time to engage in the freeing of the imprisonment of the self, its passions, and its desires.

We must spiritually awaken ourselves as soon as possible and remember all that we have forgotten - namely our true purpose in life and our connection to Allah ﷻ.

Iʿtikāf can only be called a true and dedicated *iʿtikāf* when an individual enters the masjid and re-establishes their connections from two perspectives:

1. Reconnection with the Sacred Essence of Allah ﷻ.
2. Reconnection with the Guardian of the Time - Imam al-Zamān عجّل الله تعالى فرجه الشريف.

As we know, we all originated from a drop of sperm from our father, and Allah ﷻ allowed this sperm to fertilize our mother's egg and develop into the baby that we became in the womb of our mother. Eventually, coming into this world, we realize that Allah ﷻ has given us countless abilities. Thus, an individual engaged in *iʿtikāf* must know where they came from, and through whose grace and care they came into this world, and who has provided for them during this entire journey - and that Being is none other than Allah ﷻ.

Everything which exists is due to Allah ﷻ, and in essence

Mashad, and continued to teach, eventually moving to Qum one year later.

From 1937 until very recently, he has been teaching *Fiqh* and *Uṣūl,* and is regarded as one of the senior *marājiʿ taqlīd* of the Shīʿa world.

you and I have no right to live - for this is a privilege and a blessing which He, Allah ﷻ, bestowed upon us. From the morning hours when we wake up, until the end of the day when we go to sleep, we must reflect on how much we thought about Allah ﷻ, and how much we reflected on ourselves and our origin. In addition, we must recognize that all grace we receive is due to the blessings of the one whose entire existence is purely for Allah ﷻ - and that is the saviour of humankind, Imam Walī al-ʿAṣr عج.

The highest task, and thus the best action in *iʿtikāf* is the recitation of the Quran, and the *muʿtakif* [the one engaged in *iʿtikāf*] must not neglect this important issue. As we know, *ṣalāt* is our conversation with Allah ﷻ, while recitation of the Quran is Allah's conversation with us.

If the *muʿtakif* is successful in completing the recitation of the entire Quran during the *iʿtikāf* period and asks Allah ﷻ to confer the rewards of this recitation to the Imam of the Time عج, then this gift to the 12th Imam عج is something which will actually be given to all of the Prophets ؑ that Allah ﷻ sent to guide humanity - all 124,000 of them - as the final Imam عج is the culmination of the Message of all the past Prophets ؑ.

In addition to the Quran, reciting *Ziyārat Āle Yāsīn*[9] is a

[9] *Ziyārat Āle Yāsīn* is a famous text for paying our respects to Imam al-Mahdī عج, which begins with the phrase: "Greetings be upon the progeny of Yāsīn." [سَلَامٌ عَلَى آلِ يٰسٓ] The narrator of this *Ziyārat* is Ibn ʿAbdullāh al-Himyarī who lived in the final period of the minor occultation; and several of his letters to Imam al-Mahdī عج have

been narrated; among these letters, one letter *(tawqīʿ)* contains this beautiful visitation, *Ziyārat Āle Yāsīn.*

According to the standards of documentation, the chains of transmission of this *Ziyārat* are trustworthy and authentic, and it has been reported in important sources of *ḥadīth* and supplication. According to some scholars, this *Ziyārat* is one of the most complete and comprehensive salutation texts for Imam al-Mahdi ﷻ, and it can be recited anywhere and at any time.

This *Ziyārat* begins with twenty-three salutations: the first salutation is directed towards the progeny of Yāsīn (Prophet Muḥammad ﷺ), and the rest are salutations to Imam al-Mahdī ﷻ with various special titles. In this *Ziyārat*, some of the most important Islamic and Shīʿa beliefs have been mentioned and regarded as the necessary constituents of a correct faith. Beliefs such as: Monotheism *(Tawḥīd)*, Prophethood of Prophet Muḥammad ﷺ, Divinely-appointed leadership of the twelve Imams ﷺ, reality of death, the presence of *Munkar* and *Nakīr* - the two angels who will question the souls of the deceased, the Day of Judgement, the *Ṣirāṭ* - a bridge that one must cross over to get to Paradise, Paradise, and Hell, and many more things.

After this, there are some supplications within *Ziyārat Āle Yāsīn* that are as follows: "O Allah, I request you to send salutations upon Muḥammad, the Prophet of Your mercy, and the beam of Your light, and fill my heart with the light of certainty, and my chest with the light of faith, and my mind with the light of good intentions, and my provision with the light of knowledge, and my power with the light of (proper) actions, and my tongue with the light of honesty." This eloquent *Ziyārat* concludes with expressing greetings to Imam al-Mahdī ﷻ and making supplications for his health, triumph, the closeness of his reappearance and uprising, great elixir, and everyone who takes part in *iʿtikāf* must ensure that they include the recitation of this beautiful *ziyārat* as one of the first things they engage in when they start this spiritual retreat.

Ziyārat Āle Yāsīn, as well as Sūrah Yāsīn (chapter 36) of the Quran, opens the spiritual doors to Allah ﷻ for the *muʿtakif* - and all of these pieces of guidance which we have enumerated are rooted in the Islamic teachings.

If one's *iʿtikāf* ends with these actions, then it is as if the person has come into this great act of worship with iron and leaves the masjid with gold - surely this is the power of *iʿtikāf*.

Problem Solving[10]

---

the spread of real justice on earth, the destruction of the infidels, hypocrites, and enemies of the Divine religion, and so much more.

In this *Ziyārat*, the words *ḥaqq* (truth) and *ḥujjah* (proof) have often been repeated. According to the explicit statement of some scholars, this *Ziyārat* is the most complete and comprehensive visitation of Imam al-Mahdī ﷺ that was taught by the 12th Imam himself, and many people who have had the honour of meeting the Imam has been due to a regular recitation of this beautiful *Ziyārat*.

[10] This piece was written by Āyatullāh Jawādī Āmulī, who was born in 1933 in Āmul, Iran.

He began his religious studies in the Islamic Seminary of Āmul in 1946, and completed the introductory and secondary levels of Islamic Studies in approximately five years - something which normally takes ten years to do!

In 1950, he moved to Tehran, where he studied in the Marwī Seminary for five years. In addition to the traditional subjects, he

I'tikāf in Islam is a sacred practice and an independent act of worship; and is a very important action like *ṣalāt, ḥajj,* and *'umrah.*

The guests of Allah ﷻ receive valuable gifts from the Almighty when they enter *i'tikāf,* and thus they must be in a place where others can also benefit from these gifts to be able to share them. For this reason, the believer cannot engage in this spiritual retreat in solitude where no one knows about them or what they are doing. Thus, *i'tikāf* can only be done in public - and not only in the public - but in the major centres of Islam such as Mecca, Medina, Kūfa, and Baṣra - as well as in the central masjid of a city.

I'tikāf is also valuable in solving the problems of the people and society, and it must not be that a person separates oneself from the challenges of society by engaging in the spiritual retreat [oblivious to what is going on around them].

The message of *i'tikāf* must reach the people - while the message of the people and their problems must reach Allah ﷻ through *i'tikāf* and the people engaged in it. The *mu'takif* must keep the problems of society in their mind, and sincerely pray to Allah ﷻ to alleviate the challenges of others.

---

studied Philosophy and Mysticism, and at the same time, began to teach some Seminary courses.

In 1955, he moved to Qum to continue his religious studies of learning and teaching.

Āyatullāh Jawādī Āmulī continues to live in Qum, and in addition to lecturing and being the author of hundreds of books on a wide variety of topics, he continues to guide his followers, being one of the prominent senior *marāji' taqlīd* of the Shī'a world.

After three days, at the end of the *iʿtikāf*, a *muʿtakif* should do their best not to go astray, nor should they block anyone's spiritual path. Rather, they must be such that they illuminate the spiritual aura of society - this is the cultural message of *iʿtikāf*. The issues of *ḥijāb* and chastity, and the moral problems of the society are also solved in these spiritual retreats.

We are all responsible for enjoining the good and forbidding the evil *(amr bil maʿrūf wa nahī ʿanil munkar)*, however *iʿtikāf* is like pure water which purifies the society, brings purity to the soul, and makes the society morally safe and sound. Thus, we must not think of *iʿtikāf* and those engaged in it as being done by people who are running away from their societal and religious obligations. Rather, we must realize that *iʿtikāf* is actually a way to enhance the religious progression of society.

Allah ﷻ ordered two of His Prophets- Ibrāhīm al-Khalīl ﷺ, and his son, Ismāʾīl ﷺ - to respect three groups of His guests who enter the *Ḥaram*. In addition, they were ordered to purify the sacred sanctuary specifically for the following three categories of individuals:

1. The people performing *ḥajj*.
2. Those who engage in *ṣalāt in* Masjid al-Ḥarām (the Sacred Masjid) in Mecca.
3. Those who engage in *iʿtikāf* in Masjid al-Ḥarām [as seen in the text in bold in the verse which we will quote shortly].

These two great Prophets of Allah ﷻ were ordered to rebuild and purify the masjid for these groups of individuals - one being those who want to engage in *iʿtikāf*. Allah ﷻ says in the Quran:

﴿وَإِذْ جَعَلْنَا ٱلْبَيْتَ مَثَابَةً لِّلنَّاسِ وَأَمْنًا وَٱتَّخِذُوا۟ مِن مَّقَامِ إِبْرَٰهِـۧمَ مُصَلًّى ۖ وَعَهِدْنَآ إِلَىٰٓ إِبْرَٰهِـۧمَ وَإِسْمَـٰعِيلَ أَن طَهِّرَا بَيْتِىَ لِلطَّآئِفِينَ **وَٱلْعَـٰكِفِينَ** وَٱلرُّكَّعِ ٱلسُّجُودِ ﴿١٢٥﴾﴾

> "And remember when We made the House (the Kaʿbah in Mecca) a place of return for the people, and (a refuge of) safety (a sanctuary, that is, a sign of the truth). And stand in prayer (O believers, as you did in earlier times) in the Station of Ibrāhīm *(Maqāme Ibrāhīm).* And We imposed a duty on Ibrāhīm and Ismāʾīl (saying): 'Purify My House for those who go around it as a rite of worship, **and those who abide (there) in devotion *(iʿtikāf),*** and those who bow down and prostrate (in the prayer).'"[11]

In this verse, the act of worship of *iʿtikāf* is being placed next to the major actions of worship such as *ḥajj*, *ʿumrah*, and *ṣalāt* - it is not being overshadowed by any of these three. In fact, the fasting *(ṣawm)* and praying *(ṣalāt)* are actually placed under the umbrella of *iʿtikāf,* as both are regarded as conditions for a valid *iʿtikāf.*

Iʿtikāf is one of the Divine gifts, and just as Prophet Muḥammad ﷺ gifted the act of the *tasbīḥ* of 100 *adhkār* to his beloved daughter, Fāṭima al-Zahrāʾ ﷺ - that is, saying *Allahu Akbar* - 34 times; *Alḥamdulillāh* - 33 times; and *Subḥanallāh* - 33 times, so too Allah ﷻ gifted this nation with *iʿtikāf,* so

[11] Quran, Sūrah al-Baqarah (2), Verse 125.

we must take advantage of it.

I'tikāf is so great that one of its conditions and components is fasting, and since fasting is one of the foundations of Islam - thus, they are intertwined with one another.

I'tikāf has positive and beneficial social effects, and this spiritual ceremony should be held in such a way that when people come out of this ritual, they recognize what the real Islamic System of Governance should look like.

As we know, whenever a person's fasting is valid, then their *i'tikāf* will also be valid and correct. Although one can fast anywhere and at almost any time - other than when it is not permissible to fast - however, *i'tikāf* cannot be done just anywhere: it can only take place in one of four masājid,[12] or in the central masjid of one's city.

By stressing that *i'tikāf* must only take place in the central masjid as opposed to merely any masjid in the city in which one lives, Islam wants to impress upon the believers that this spiritual retreat is not simply performed in any building in which people congregate for the daily prayers. Rather, this has to be a specific place - it must be a masjid where all of the people, or at least most of the Muslim community attend for the daily congregational prayers, and as such, these masājid hold a greater importance in the sight of Allah ﷻ.

---

[12] These four masājid include: Masjid al-Ḥarām in Mecca, Arabia; Masjid al-Nabawī in Medina, Arabia; the Grand Masjid of Kūfa in the city of Kūfa, Iraq; and the Grand Masjid of Baṣra in the city of Baṣra, Iraq.

An Act of Worship Similar to Ḥajj[13]

In the noisy world of materialism, where the attraction is towards avariciousness, rust settles on the heart and soul of a believer: a rust of neglect and physical distance from Allah ﷻ, which if not removed by prayer *(ṣalāt)* and worship *(ʿibādah)*, may annihilate any remaining presence of spirituality from an individual.

In the *aḥādīth*, *ṣalāt* is likened to a stream of clean water in which a person washes oneself five times a day - and this is reference to the point we made about the necessity to ensure that we clean off any rust from our heart before it is too late.

Among the acts of worship, *iʿtikāf* has a special feature; and in some ways, it is like *ḥajj* and the *iḥrām* ceremonies. Just as once a person enters the state of *iḥrām*, many things

---

[13] This piece was written by Āyatullāh Nāṣir Makārim Shīrāzī who was born in 1927 in Shīrāz, Iran.

After completing his primary and secondary education, he began his religious education at the age of fourteen in Shīrāz and then entered the Seminary in Qum.

In 1950, he moved to Najaf, however, after one year of education, he to return back to Qum. In Najaf, he participated in the classes of the late Āyatullāh Abūl Qāsim al-Khuʾī ؒ, and the late Āyatullāh Muḥsin al-Ḥakīm ؒ. At the age of twenty-four, he received the permission for *ijtihād.*

Āyatullāh Nāṣir Makārim Shīrāzī continues to live in Qum and teaches students on a regular basis. He is a prolific researcher and author having hundreds of titles to his name including many of which are now available in English. He also continues to guide the Shīʿa community, being one of the senior *marājiʿ taqlīd.*

which are normally permissible become impermissible *(ḥarām)* - similarly, when one enters *iʿtikāf,* a number of things become impermissible for the *muʿtakif,* which lead a person to a direction full of spirituality.

Staying in the precinct of a masjid for three days, fasting and worshipping, striving for self-improvement, and not thinking about anything other than Allah ﷻ creates a massive transformation in the human soul, and provides a type of spiritual clarity and illumination which are unique.

By the blessings of Allah ﷻ, in recent years, *iʿtikāf* has been welcomed even by the young people of the society, especially our dear students, and they have understood the spiritual pleasures and powerful effects of this transcendent act of worship, and we congratulate them on this great understanding and awakening.

We hope that the dear youth, especially the students, will be pioneers in the performance of *iʿtikāf,* and will be able to keep its importance alive in our society, as this is one of the most effective means of getting closer to Allah ﷻ, and without a doubt, they will fully benefit from its spiritual results.

From my part, I am grateful for the efforts of those involved [in the planning and execution] as they have provided the prerequisites for performing this important act of worship of the Divine; and may Allah ﷻ bless them all for their efforts.

Do Not Limit Iʿtikāf to the Month of Rajab[14]

We must realize that *iʿtikāf* should not be limited strictly to the month of Rajab, but rather, this magnificent ceremony of *iʿtikāf* should also be held in the month of Shaʿbān and the month of Ramaḍān as well.

As we know from the historical texts, Prophet Muḥammad ﷺ used to retreat to the masjid for *iʿtikāf* for ten days every year, separating himself from the people, and devoting himself to praying to Allah ﷻ.

During the minimum three days of *iʿtikāf*, believers who are engaged in this act of worship must focus only on praying to Allah ﷻ, and avoid this transient world, and all worldly matters.

Again, I reiterate this point that we must **not** limit *iʿtikāf* to the month of Rajab and should try to perform it during the

---

[14] This piece was written by Āyatullāh Jaʿfar Subḥānī, who was born in 1926 in the city of Tabriz, Iran. After completing his primary school and the introductory studies, Āyatullāh Subḥānī went on to study the books of Persian literature and grammar.

In 1940, he proceeded to enter the Theological Seminary of Tabriz and completed the preliminary and second level of studies there. In four short years - something which normally takes ten years - he began the highest level of Islamic Studies in *Fiqh* and *Uṣūl*.

He continues to teach the various Islamic Sciences in Qum, and is also a prolific researcher and author, having written hundreds of titles in Arabic and Farsi on areas of exegesis of the Noble Quran, Islamic Theology, Jurisprudence, and contemporary topics such as Islam and Religious Pluralism, Apostacy, and many more - some of which are available in English.

month of Shaʿbān and the month of Ramaḍān as well.

Yes, it is true that *iʿtikāf* during the month of Rajab is highly virtuous, and those blessed to perform this act of devotion focus on self-improvement and avoid any sins during these three days, however we must expand the scope of *iʿtikāf* in our society.

A country whose youths are religiously transformed and can increase their spirituality will become the future hope for the further development and advancement of that country.

My advice to the dear brothers and sisters who are engaging in *iʿtikāf* all around the world is that they should not waste their precious time merely eating when it is permitted to eat in the evening [after *maghrib*], and that too, they must not eat excessively, or busy themselves with excessive sleep during these three days.

Rather, they must try to separate themselves from worldly affairs and engage in worship. During these days and nights, they must try to remember the martyrs who gave their lives for the sake of Islam and for the nation. They must know that if the blessings of the ability to perform the *iʿtikāf* become even more popular in this country (Iran), then it is all thanks to the blood of the martyrs.

Final Words

In the sacred tapestry of worship within Islam, the act of *iʿtikāf* emerges as a luminous thread, weaving through the fabric of devotion and spiritual introspection.

As we conclude this introduction which offered a comprehensive exploration into the profound significance of *iʿtikāf*, it is incumbent upon us to reflect upon the transformative power it holds within the hearts of believers.

As you will see, throughout the chapters of this book, we have tried out best to traverse the depths of this sacred tradition, trying our best to unveil layers of meaning and spiritual enrichment that accompany the observance of *iʿtikāf*.

At its core, *iʿtikāf* beckons the soul to retreat from the clamour of worldly distractions, creating a sacred space for an intimate communion with the Divine. The seclusion within a masjid during this devoted period offers a unique opportunity for believers to draw closer to Allah ﷻ, engage in profound self-reflection, and immerse themselves in the serene ambiance of spiritual growth. Physical withdrawal from this world symbolizes a spiritual renaissance, a conscious effort to detach from the mundane, and delve into the ethereal realms of worship and contemplation.

The importance of *iʿtikāf* transcends the temporal boundaries of its observance, resonating with timeless wisdom that extends beyond the confines of a specific period in the Islamic calendar. It serves as a testament of a believer's commitment to deepening their relationship with Allah ﷻ, embodying the essence of submission, surrender, and unwavering faith. The sequestered moments within a masjid become a sanctuary for introspection, prayer, and connection with the Quran, paving the way for a profound spiritual metamorphosis.

Throughout this book, we have endeavoured to unravel the layers of significance embedded in *iʿtikāf*, and the spiritual benefits that await those who embark on this sacred journey. The wisdom and guidance distilled within these pages aim to illuminate the path for believers seeking a deeper understanding of this noble act of worship, enriching their spiritual repertoire, and fostering a more profound connection with their Creator.

In compiling this book, the final section which makes up the Juristic rulings have been extracted and translated from the most recent edition of *The Comprehensive Manual of Islamic Laws (Tawḍīḥ al-Masāʾil Jāmiʿ)* of Āyatullāh Sayyid ʿAlī al-Ḥusaynī al-Sīstānī, as found on his official website, www.sistani.org.[15]

We have done our best to make this translation as simple and fluid as possible, and as Āyatullāh al-Sīstānī refers to various other rulings found in his four-volume *Islamic Laws Manual,* not available in English, we have also translated those portions to ensure that the ones engaging in *iʿtikāf* have access to all of the latest rulings for this great act of worship.

Although we have maintained all of the key terminologies of Islamic Jurisprudence in their original Arabic, we have provided translations and explanations as required.

In addition, we have renumbered the rulings starting at **Issue 1** and have not retained the actual **Issue Number** for the rulings presented by Āyatullāh al-Sīstānī (to avoid confusion).

We have done our best to maintain the integrity of the original text in our translation, however, where the original

---

[15] Found on: www.sistani.org/persian/book/fatwā/ - Last accessed on March 22, 2023.

Persian text is worded in such a way that it presupposes that the reader has the requisite knowledge of other sections of Islamic Laws, we have taken the liberty to add an explanation in square brackets, and as required, in the footnotes. Some areas required further clarification for which we sought guidance directly from the liaison office of Āyatullāh al-Sīstānī.

It is obvious that as human beings, we are fallible and make mistakes, thus, if you spot any errors in this work, then please contact us at **iph@iph.ca** so that we can resolve these issues for future reprints or online hosting.

The research, writing, translation, compilation, and publishing of this book would not have been possible without the constant flow of blessings of Allah ﷻ which He constantly showers upon this non-descript.

In addition, it is through the inspiration and support of the Final Prophet, Muḥammad ﷺ, and the immaculate leaders of this faith, his Ahlul Bayt ﷵ, that we were able to even engage in such a project.

Having these sources of guidance and being able to access the pristine teachings thanks to the selfless efforts of the scholars of this faith who have given their blood, sweat, and tears over the past 1,200 years by preserving and carrying the teachings forward has allowed us to have a greater glimpse into the beauty of the teachings of Islam.

Next, it is through the meticulous efforts of our esteemed editor, Arifa Hudda, that this book has gone from conception to reality. Her commitment to excellence, keen editorial insight, and dedication to preserving the authenticity and clarity of the content have been invaluable throughout this journey. Her contributions to this and other work is a testament of her passion for facilitating the dissemination of knowledge and spiritual insights - a formidable task which she has been carrying out for almost 25 years.

In extending our sincere gratitude, we also acknowledge the instrumental role played by our generous donors - who wished to remain anonymous - whose benevolence has paved the way for the publication of this book. Their commitment to supporting endeavours which promote understanding, unity, and spiritual growth is truly commendable. It is through their generosity that this book found its way into the hands of readers, serving as a beacon of knowledge and inspiration for those seeking to deepen their connection with Allah ﷻ through the practice of *iʿtikāf.*

As we conclude this literary expedition, let us carry forward the wisdom garnered from these pages into our lives, transforming knowledge into action, and contemplation into devotion. May the insights shared within the chapters of this book serve as a source of guidance and inspiration for those embarking on the Sacred Journey of *Iʿtikāf and* may the echoes of their devotion resonate in the chambers of their hearts, drawing them nearer to Allah ﷻ.

May this book - born from a collective effort and guided by the light of knowledge - be a source of blessings for all those who engage in its teachings. May it inspire a revival of the spirit, a rekindling of faith, and a steadfast commitment to the timeless practice of *iʿtikāf.*

فَاذْكُرُونِي أَذْكُرْكُمْ
وَاشْكُرُوا لِي وَلَا تَكْفُرُونِ

"So always remember and make mention of Me, that I may remember and make mention of you; and give thanks to Me, and do not be ungrateful to Me."

Quran, Sūrah al-Baqarah (2), Verse 152

Saleem Bhimji
Director of the Islamic Publishing House
February 8th, 2024 CE • 27th of Rajab, 1445 AH
Mabʿath of Prophet Muḥammad ﷺ
Richmond, BC, Canada

Forty Ḥadīth about Spiritual Seclusion[16]

What follows in this section is a collection of forty *aḥādīth* in regard to *iʿtikāf* and other related topics of spiritual seclusion. We have included the Arabic text of the *ḥadīth* in the footnotes.

1. Imam ʿAlī al-Riḍā ﵇ said: "One night spent in *iʿtikāf* in the month of Ramaḍān is equivalent to performing one *ḥajj*; and one night spent in *iʿtikāf* in the Masjid of the Messenger of Allah ﷺ at his grave is equivalent to performing one *ḥajj* and one *ʿumrah*."[17]

2. Imam Jaʿfar al-Ṣādiq ﵇ said: "A wise person ... should divide their time into certain portions: a portion of time for conversing with one's Lord, the Mighty and Glorious; a portion of time for self-accountability; a portion of time for

---

[16] Extracted from: https://www.ziaossalehin.ir/fa/content/17729 - last accessed on February 3, 2024.

[17] *Biḥār al-Anwār*, Vol. 98, Pg. 151:

إِعْتِكَافُ لَيْلَةٍ فِي شَهْرِ رَمَضَانَ يَعْدِلُ حَجَّةً وَإِعْتِكَافُ لَيْلَةٍ فِي مَسْجِدِ رَسُولِ اللّٰهِ ﷺ وَعِنْدَ قَبْرِهِ يَعْدِلُ حَجَّةً وَعُمْرَةً.

contemplating upon what Allah, the Mighty and Glorious, has created for that person; and a portion of time to be alone, enjoying the lawful pleasures of one's soul."[18]

3. Ibn Mahrān has reported: "I was sitting with Imam Ḥasan (a) in the masjid during *iʿtikāf* when a man came and said: 'O son of the Prophet! So-and-so is demanding money from me and wants to imprison me for non-payment.'

Imam Ḥasan (a) replied: 'By Allah! I do not have any money to help pay your debt.'

The man said: 'Then talk to my debtor (to give me an extension).'

Imam Ḥasan (a) was preparing to leave (the masjid), so I said: 'O son of the Messenger of Allah! Have you forgotten that you are in the midst of *iʿtikāf*, and you cannot leave the masjid?'

He replied: 'I have not forgotten. Rather, I have heard from my father, who heard it from my grandfather, the Messenger of Allah, that he said: 'Whoever strives to fulfill the need of one's Muslim brother (or sister), it is as if they have observed fasts for a thousand years and spent their nights in worship for a thousand years.'"[19]

---

[18] *Al-Khiṣāl*, Vol. 2, Pg. 525:
عَلَىٰ الْعَاقِلِ ... أَنْ يَكُونَ لَهُ سَاعَاتٌ: سَاعَةٌ يُنَاجِي فِيهَا رَبَّهُ عَزَّ وَجَلَّ وَسَاعَةٌ يُحَاسِبُ نَفْسَهُ وَسَاعَةٌ يَتَفَكَّرُ فِيمَا صَنَعَ اللّٰهُ عَزَّ وَجَلَّ إِلَيْهِ وَسَاعَةٌ يَخْلُو فِيهَا بِحَظِّ نَفْسِهِ مِنَ الْحَلَالَ.

[19] *Al-Faqīh*, Vol. 2, Pg. 189.

4. Imam ʿAlī ﷺ said: "Looking at a scholar is more beloved to Allah than observing *iʿtikāf* for an entire year in the Sacred House *(Kaʿbah)*."[20]

5. Prophet Muḥammad ﷺ said: "O Abū Dharr! Surely Allah, the Exalted, grants you, as long as you sit in the masjid, a degree in Paradise for every breath you take. The angels send blessings upon you; and for every breath you take, ten good deeds are written for you, while ten sins are erased from you."[21]

6. Prophet Muḥammad ﷺ said: "A person who returns from the masjid does not do so with less than one of three things [being given to them]: Either a prayer through which Allah admits them to Paradise, or a supplication through which Allah averts worldly afflictions from them, or a brother/sister who benefits them in the way of Allah, the Mighty and Glorious."[22]

---

[20] *Mustadrak al-Wasāʾil*, Vol. 9, Pg. 153:
أَلنَّظَرُ إِلَىٰ الْعَالِمِ أَحَبُّ إِلَىٰ اللّٰهِ مِنْ إِعْتِكَافِ سَنَةٍ فِي الْبَيْتِ الْحَرَامِ.

[21] *Biḥār al-Anwār*, Vol. 74, Pg. 86:
يَا أَبَا ذَرٍّ: إِنَّ اللّٰهَ تَعَالَىٰ يُعْطِيكَ مَا دُمْتَ جَالِسًا فِي الْمَسْجِدِ بِكُلِّ نَفَسٍ تَنَفَّسْتَ دَرَجَةً فِي الْجَنَّةِ وَتُصَلِّي عَلَيْكَ الْمَلَائِكَةُ وَيُكْتَبُ لَكَ بِكُلِّ نَفَسٍ تَنَفَّسْتَ فِيهِ عَشْرُ حَسَنَاتٍ وَتُمْحَى عَنْكَ عَشْرُ سَيِّئَاتٍ.

[22] *Al-Amālī* by Shaykh al-Ṭūsī, Pg. 46:
لَا يَرْجِعُ صَاحِبُ الْمَسْجِدِ بِأَقَلَّ مِنْ إِحْدَىٰ ثَلَاثٍ: إِمَّا دُعَاءٍ يَدْعُو بِهِ يُدْخِلُهُ اللّٰهُ بِهِ الْجَنَّةَ وَإِمَّا دُعَاءٍ يَدْعُو بِهِ لِيَصْرِفَ اللّٰهُ بِهِ عَنْهُ بَلَاءَ الدُّنْيَا وَإِمَّا أَخٍ يَسْتَفِيدُهُ فِي اللّٰهِ عَزَّ وَجَلَّ.

7. Prophet Muḥammad ﷺ said: "A man sitting with his wife and children is more beloved to Allah than observing *iʿtikāf* for a year in this masjid of mine (the Masjid of the Prophet ﷺ in Medina)."[23]

8. Prophet Muḥammad ﷺ said: "All of humanity are the dependents of Allah, the All-High. The most beloved among them to Allah is the one who benefits the dependents of Allah, or brings happiness to my household, or walks with a Muslim brother (or sister) to fulfill their need, which is more beloved to Allah than observing *iʿtikāf* for two months in the Sacred Masjid [in Mecca]."[24]

9. Imam ʿAlī said: "Indeed he [the Prophet of Allah ﷺ] used to seclude himself in [the cave of] Ḥirā every year, and I would see him while no one else saw him."[25]

10. Imam ʿAlī said: "A person [who partakes] in *iʿtikāf* must remain in a masjid, and engage in the remembrance of

---

[23] *Majmūʿatul Warrām*, Vol. 2, Pg. 121
جُلُوسُ الْـمَرْءِ عِنْدَ عِيَالِهِ أَحَبُّ إِلَىٰ اللهِ تَعَالَىٰ مِنْ إِعْتِكَافٍ فِي مَسْجِدِي هٰذَا.

[24] *Biḥār al-Anwār*, Vol. 71, Pg. 316:
أَلْخَلْقُ عِيَالُ الله تَعَالَىٰ فَأَحَبُّ الْخَلْقِ إِلَىٰ اللهِ مَنْ نَفَعَ عِيَالَ اللهِ وَ أَدْخَلَ عَلَىٰ أَهْلِ بَيْتِي سُرُورًا وَمَشْيٌ مَعَ أَخٍ مُسْلِمٍ فِي حَاجَةٍ أَحَبُّ إِلَىٰ اللهِ تَعَالَىٰ مِنْ إِعْتِكَافِ شَهْرَيْنِ فِي الْـمَسْجِدِ الْحَرَامِ.

[25] *Nahj al-Balāgha*, Pg. 300:
وَلَقَدْ كَانَ [رَسُولُ اللهِ ﷺ] يُجَاوِرُ فِي كُلِّ سَنَةٍ بِحِرَاءَ فَأَرَاهُ وَلَا يَرَاهُ غَيْرِي.

Allah, recitation of the Quran, and *ṣalāt*."[26]

11. Prophet Muḥammad ﷺ said: "The best of people are the ones who love worship, embrace it, love it with their heart, engage in it with their body, and devote themselves to it."[27]

12. Imam Mūsā al-Kāẓim ؑ prayed to Allāh ﷻ saying: "O Allah! You know that I had asked You to provide me with a place of seclusion for Your worship, and You have done so - and so, to You belongs all praise!"[28]

13. Imam Jaʿfar al-Ṣādiq ؑ said: "The Battle of Badr took place in the month of Ramaḍān, so the Messenger of Allah could not observe *iʿtikāf* (that year). Then, when it was possible for him, he observed *iʿtikāf* for twenty days - ten days for that current year and ten days as compensation for the previous year [in which he missed the *iʿtikāf*]."[29]

14. Imam Jaʿfar al-Ṣādiq ؑ said: "It is appropriate for the one

---

[26] *Mustadrak al-Wasāʾil*, Vol. 7, Pg. 564:
يَلْزَمُ الْـمُعْتَكِفُ الْـمَسْجِدَ وَيَلْزَمُ ذِكْرَ اللّٰهِ وَتِلَاوَةَ الْقُرآنِ وَالصَّلَاةَ.

[27] *Wasāʾil al-Shīʿa*, Vol. 1, Pg. 83:
أَفْضَلُ النَّاسِ مَنْ عَشِقَ الْعِبَادَةَ فَعَانَقَهَا وَأَحَبَّهَا بِقَلْبِهِ وَبَاشَرَهَا بِجَسَدِهِ وَتَفَرَّغَ لَهَا...

[28] *Al-Irshād*, Vol. 2, Pg. 240:
أَللّٰهُمَّ إِنَّكَ تَعْلَمُ إِنِّي كُنْتُ أَسْأَلُكَ أَنْ تُفَرِّغَنِي لِعِبَادَتِكَ. أَللّٰهُمَّ وَقَدْ فَعَلْتَ فَلَكَ الْحَمْدُ.

[29] *Al-Kāfī*, Vol. 4, Pg. 175:
كَانَتْ بَدْرٌ فِي شَهْرِ رَمَضَانَ فَلَمْ يَعْتَكِفْ رَسُولَ اللّٰهِ ﷺ فَلَمَّا أَنْ كَانَ مِنْ قَابِلٍ إِعْتَكَفَ عَشْرَيْنَ عَشْرًا لِعَامِهِ وَعَشْرًا قَضَاءً لِمَا فَاتَهُ.

who intends to observe *iʿtikāf* to stipulate a condition [in their intention that if a challenge comes up in their life necessitating that they come out of the state of *iʿtikāf,* then they will do so, otherwise it is not permissible to leave the state of *iʿtikāf*], just as the one entering a state of *iḥrām* should stipulate a condition when they enter into the state of *iḥrām* [and make a similar intention]."[30]

15. Imam Jaʿfar al-Ṣādiq ﵇ said: "In the Torah, it is written: 'O son of Adam! Devote yourself to My worship, and I will fill your heart with richness without you asking Me, and thus, I will make it incumbent upon Myself to fulfill your requests.'"[31]

16. Prophet Muḥammad ﷺ said: "A person [engaged] in *iʿtikāf* should refrain from sins, and for that person - the doer of good deeds - all the rewards flow."[32]

17. Prophet Muḥammad ﷺ said: "The first day [of three] in which the person observes *iʿtikāf* seeking the countenance of Allah, the Almighty, Allah will create three trenches between

---

[30] *Al-Kāfī*, Vol. 4, Pg. 177:
يَنْبَغِي لِلْمُعْتَكِفِ إِذَا اعْتَكَفَ أَنْ يَشْتَرِطَ كَمَا يَشْتَرِطُ الَّذِي يُحْرِمُ.

[31] Ibid., Vol. 2, Pg. 83:
فِي التَّوْرَاةِ مَكْتُوبٌ يَا ابْنَ آدَمَ تَفَرَّغْ لِعِبَادَتِي أَمْلَأْ قَلْبَكَ غِنًى وَلَا أَكِلْكَ إِلَىٰ طَلَبِكَ وَعَلَيَّ أَنْ أَسُدَّ فَاقَتَكَ...

[32] *Kanz al-ʿUmmāl*, Vol. 8, Pg. 531:
أَلْمُعْتَكِفُ يَعْكِفُ الذُّنُوبَ وَيَجْرِي لَهُ مِنَ الْأَجْرِ عَامِلِ الْحَسَنَاتِ كُلِّهَا.

them and the Hellfire."[33]

18. Prophet Muḥammad ﷺ said: "Sitting in the masjid while waiting for the prayer is worship, as long as nothing inappropriate happens." It was asked: "O Messenger of Allah! What is considered inappropriate?" He replied: "Engaging in gossiping *(ghībah)*."[34]

19. Imam Muḥammad al-Bāqir ؑ said: "A person [engaged] in *iʿtikāf* ... must not argue [with others], buy, or sell [anything]."[35]

20. Imam Muḥammad al-Bāqir ؑ said: "A person [engaged] in *iʿtikāf* must not smell perfumes or take delight in the fragrance of scents."[36]

21. Imam Jaʿfar al-Ṣādiq ؑ said: "*Iʿtikāf* is not appropriate except in a congregational masjid."[37]

---

[33] *Kanz al-ʿUmmāl*, Vol. 8, Pg. 532:
مَنِ اعْتَكَفَ يَوْمًا ابْتِغَاءَ وَجْهِ اللّٰهِ عَزَّوَجَلَّ جَعَلَ اللّٰهُ بَيْنَهُ وَبَيْنَ النَّارِ ثَلَاثَةَ خَنَادِقَ.

[34] *Biḥār al-Anwār*, Vol. 80, Pg. 384:
أَلْجُلُوسُ فِي الْمَسْجِدِ لِإِنْتِظَارِ الصَّلَاةِ عِبَادَةٌ مَا لَمْ يَحْدِثْ. قِيلَ: يَا رَسُولَ اللّٰهِ وَمَا الْحَدَثُ؟ قَالَ: أَلْإِغْتِيَابُ.

[35] *Man la Yaḥdhuruhu al-Faqīh*, Vol. 2, Pg. 186:
أَلْمُعْتَكِفُ ... لَا يُمَارَى وَلَا يَشْتَرِي وَلَا يَبِيعُ.

[36] Ibid.:
أَلْمُعْتَكِفُ لَا يَشَمُّ الطِّيبَ وَلَا يَتَلَذَّذُ بِالرَّيْحَانَ.

[37] *Al-Tahdhīb*, Vol. 4, Pg. 290:

22. Imam Jaʿfar al-Ṣādiq (ع) said: "It is not suitable for a person [engaged] in *iʿtikāf* to leave the masjid except for a necessary need [absolute necessity] that cannot be avoided."[38]

23. Imam Jaʿfar al-Ṣādiq (ع) said: "*Iʿtikāf* cannot be less than three days."[39]

24. Sufyān al-Thawrī narrated: "I had the honour of being in the presence of Imam Jaʿfar al-Ṣādiq (ع), so I asked him: 'O son of the Messenger of Allah! Why have you distanced yourselves from the people?' He replied: 'O Sufyān! Times have become corrupted, and people have changed, so I found solitude and seclusion to bring peace to my heart.'"[40]

25. Prophet Muḥammad ﷺ said: "Whoever observes *iʿtikāf* with true devotion and faith - seeking rewards, will be forgiven for their past sins."[41]

26. Prophet Muḥammad ﷺ said: "Every sitting in the masjid

لَا يَكُونُ إِعْتِكَافٌ إِلَّا فِي مَسْجِدِ جَمَاعَةٍ.

[38] *Man la Yaḥḍhuruhu al-Faqīh*, Vol. 2, Pg. 187:
لَا يَنْبَغِي لِلْمُعْتَكِفِ أَنْ يَخْرُجَ مِنَ الْمَسْجِدِ إِلَّا لِحَاجَةٍ لَا بُدَّ مِنهَا.

[39] *Al-Kāfī*, Vol. 4, Pg. 177:
لَا يَكُونُ الْإِعْتِكَافُ أَقَلَّ مِنْ ثَلَاثَةِ أَيَّامٍ.

[40] *Biḥār al-Anwār*, Vol. 47, Pg. 60:
يَا سُفْيَانَ! فَسَدَ الزَّمَانُ وَتَغَيَّرَ الْإِخْوَانُ، فَرَأَيْتُ الْإِنْفِرَادَ أَسْكَنَ لِلْفُؤَادِ.

[41] *Kanz al-Ummāl*, Ḥadīth 24007:
مَنِ اعْتَكَفَ إِيمَانًا وَاحْتِسَابًا غُفِرَ لَهُ مَا تَقَدَّمَ مِنْ ذَنْبِهِ.

is vain except for three [instances]: recitation by a person performing one's *ṣalāt*, [being engaged in the] remembrance of Allah, and the one seeking knowledge."[42]

27. Imam ʿAlī ﷺ said: "How can a person find the pleasure of worship if they do not refrain from following their base desires?"[43]

28. Imam ʿAlī ﷺ said: "Servitude consists of five things: emptying the stomach, reciting the Quran, standing in prayer at night, humbly supplicating at dawn, and crying out of the fear of Allah."[44]

29. Imam Jaʿfar al-Ṣādiq ﷺ said: "I recommend you visit the masājid, for they are the houses of Allah on Earth. Whoever comes to them in a state of purity, Allah will purify them from their sins, and count them among His visitors. Therefore, increase your prayers and supplications in them."[45]

---

[42] *Biḥār al-Anwār*, Vol. 77, Pg. 88; *Mizān al-Ḥikmah*, Ḥadīth 8304:
كُلُّ جُلوسٍ فِي الْمَسْجِدِ لَغوٌ إِلَّا ثَلَاثَةً: قِرَاءَةُ مُصَلٍّ أَوْ ذِكْرُ اللهِ أَوْ سَائِلٌ عَنْ عِلْمٍ.

[43] *Ghurar al-Ḥikam*, Pg. 199, Ḥadīth 3938:
كَيْفَ يَجِدُ لَذَّةَ الْعِبَادَةِ مَنْ لَا يَصُومُ عَنِ الْهَوىٰ.

[44] *Mustadrak al-Wasā'il*, Vol. 11, Pg. 244, Ḥadīth 12875; *Mizān al-Ḥikmah*, Ḥadīth 354:
أَلْعُبُودِيَّةُ خَمْسَةُ أَشْيَاءَ: خَلَاءُ الْبَطْنِ، وَقِرَاءَةُ الْقُرْآنِ، وَقِيَامُ اللَّيلِ، وَالتَّضَرُّعُ عِندَ الصُّبْحِ، وَالْبُكَاءُ مِنْ خَشْيَةِ اللهِ.

[45] *Al-Amālī* by Shaykh al-Ṣadūq, Pg. 293:

30. Imam ʿAlī ؑ said: "Settle in your hearts the recognition of the One whom you worship, so that the worship of your limbs benefits you in moving towards the worship of the One you know."[46]

31. Imam ʿAlī ؑ said: "Choosing seclusion is the habit of the righteous ones."[47]

32. Imam Jaʿfar al-Ṣādiq ؑ said: "When the last ten days of the month of Ramaḍān would arrive, the Messenger of Allah ﷺ would perform *iʿtikāf* in the masjid. A canopy of animal skin was set up for him, and he would tighten his belt (not engage in anything that would distract him from Allah ﷻ - especially martial relationships) and fold his bed (engage in more worship and less sleep)."[48]

عَلَيْكُمْ بِإِتْيَانِ الْمَسَاجِدِ فَإِنَّهَا بُيُوتُ اللهِ فِي الْأَرْضِ وَمَنْ أَتَاهَا مُتطَهِّرًا طَهَّرَهُ اللهُ مِنْ ذُنُوبِهِ وَكُتِبَ مِنْ زَوَّارِهِ فأَكْثِرُوا فِيهَا مِنَ الصَّلَاةِ وَالدُّعَاءِ.

[46] *Biḥār al-Anwār*, Vol. 75, Pg. 63:
سَكِّنُوا فِي أَنْفُسِكُمْ مَعْرِفَةَ مَا تَعْبُدُونَ حَتَّى يَنْفَعَكُمْ مَا تُحَرِّكُونَ مِنَ الْجَوَارِحِ بِعِبَادَةِ مَنْ تَعْرِفُونَ.

[47] *Ghurar al-Ḥikam*, Pg. 318:
مُلَازَمَةُ الْخَلْوَةِ دَأْبُ الصُّلَحَاءِ.

[48] *Al-Kāfī*, Vol. 4, Pg. 175:
كَانَ رَسُولُ اللهِ ﷺ إِذَا كَانَ الْعَشْرُ الْأَوَاخِرُ اعْتَكَفَ فِي الْمَسْجِدِ وَضُرِبَتْ لَهُ قُبَّةٌ مِنْ شَعْرٍ وَشَمَّرَ الْمِئْزَرَ وَطَوَى فِرَاشَهُ.

33. Prophet Muḥammad ﷺ said: "The *i'tikāf* of ten days in the month of Ramaḍān is equal to two *ḥajj* and two *'umrah*."[49]

34. Imam 'Alī al-Sajjād ؏ said: "Fasting during *i'tikāf* is obligatory."[50]

35. Imam 'Alī al-Sajjād ؏ prayed to Allah ﷻ saying: "Adorn for me the exclusivity of conversing with You both day and night."[51]

36. Um Sa'īd reported that she asked Imam Ja'far al-Ṣādiq ؏ about the reward of visiting Imam Ḥusayn ؏, to which he replied: "It is equal to one *ḥajj* and one *'umrah*, two months of *i'tikāf* in the Sacred Masjid, fasting during those months, and actually, it is even better than that."[52]

37. Imam 'Alī ؏ said: "Attaining righteousness and virtue lies in distancing oneself from the people of this world."[53]

---

[49] *Al-Faqīh*, Vol. 2, Pg. 188:

إِعْتِكَافُ عَشْرٍ فِي شَهْرِ رَمَضَانَ يَعْدِلُ حَجَّتَيْنِ وَعُمْرَتَيْنِ.

[50] *Al-Kāfī*, Vol. 4, Pg. 83:

صَوْمُ الْإِعْتِكَافِ وَاجِبٌ.

[51] *Ṣaḥīfa Sajjādiya*, Pg. 224:

وَزَيِّنْ لِي التَّفَرُّدَ بِـمُنَاجَاتِكَ بِاللَّيْلِ وَالنَّهَارِ...

[52] *Wasāʾil al-Shīʿa*, Vol. 14, Pg. 436:

تَعْدِلُ حَجَّةً وَعُمْرَةً وَاعْتِكَافَ شَهْرَيْنِ فِي الْمَسْجِدِ الْحَرَامِ وَصِيَامَهَا وَخَيْرٌ مِنْهَا كَذَا...

[53] *Mustadrak al-Wasāʾil*, Vol. 11, Pg. 393:

فِي اعْتِزَالِ أَبْنَاءِ الدُّنْيَا جِمَاعُ الصَّلَاحِ.

38. Imam ʿAlī ﷺ said: "Safety lies in solitude."[54]

39. Imam ʿAlī ﷺ said: "One who withdraws from people will find intimacy with Allah, the Exalted."[55]

40. Imam ʿAlī ﷺ said: "Seclusion is the fortified fortress of God-consciousness *(taqwā)*."[56]

---

[54] *Mustadrak al-Wasāʾil*, Vol. 11, Pg. 393:

أَلسَّلَامَةُ فِي التَّفَرُّدِ.

[55] Ibid.:

مَنْ إِنْفَرَدَ عَنِ النَّاسِ أَنِسَ بِاللّٰهِ سُبْحَانَهُ.

[56] Ibid.:

أَلْعُزْلَةُ حِصْنُ التَّقْوَى.

The Wisdom of Iʿtikāf[57]

One of the blessings of the Islamic Revolution in Iran is the enthusiasm of the people towards religion [and more specifically, the pure and pristine teachings of Islam as taught by Prophet Muḥammad ﷺ and the Ahlul Bayt عليهم السلام in the realm of spirituality], and more specifically, the youth, toward the act of worship of the *iʿtikāf* [which has not only impacted the youth in this one country but has actually taken shape around the world].

Undoubtedly, this enthusiasm reflects the spirituality of the youth and the people of this land [and elsewhere in regions that have been impacted by the spiritual guidance of the Prophet Muḥammad ﷺ and the Ahlul Bayt عليهم السلام] and demonstrates that this form of worship has been well-received, and as we know, each and every act of worship in Islam also brings certain blessings along with it.

This passion and ever-developing trend occurs, while at the same time, a wave of false mysticism *[pseudo-ʿirfān]* is on the rise. It also comes at a time when the emergence of the young generation's inclinations [to their base desires] have

---

57 Written by Sayyid Maḥmūd Ṭāhirī, found on: www.ziaossalehin.ir/fa/content/1095.

increasingly stimulated them and targeted them through enticing advertisements through satellite television, Internet, and other forms of mass communication, dragging them towards various illicit indulgences.

Thus, an enthusiasm towards *iʿtikāf* - in addition to serving as an antidote to the spiritual dangers and temptations - is a clear call to the rejection of the prevailing trend of inappropriate inclinations and signals a growth in spirituality among the current generation.

Although on the surface, the fruits of *iʿtikāf* are individual based, and it is the individual who achieves self-improvement and self-discipline through participation in the spiritual atmosphere which permeates *iʿtikāf*, it is essential to remember that social reform always begins with individuals.

In this way, *iʿtikāf* demonstrates its blessings and benefits at a societal level and compels society to move towards goodness and righteousness.

From this perspective, it can be said that if *iʿtikāf* is carried out correctly, and the programs are safeguarded from all spiritual pitfalls that may plague it if not carefully planned and executed, it can be transformed into a social movement - a constructive and leading movement that can become one of the tools of cultural development in society.

Iʿtikāf in Terminology and Jurisprudence

Technically speaking, *iʿtikāf* is defined as: "devotion, dedication, and turning one's attention to something out of respect; devoting oneself to something in a way that it cannot be turned away from; staying in one place for some time and restricting oneself to a particular place for a certain period."[58]

However, in the context of Islamic Jurisprudence, *iʿtikāf* is defined as: "a devotion of three days or more in a masjid with the intention of seeking nearness to Allah ﷻ, accompanied by specific acts of worship while maintaining certain Jurisprudential conditions."[59]

Iʿtikāf in the terminology of the mystics *(ʿurafāʾ)* and those on the path of spiritual development is further defined as "emptying the heart of worldly preoccupations and submitting oneself to the Lord." It has been said by the spiritual masters that *iʿtikāf* is "choosing to stay," and its meaning is that "As long as I do not achieve forgiveness from You, I will not move away from Your threshold, O Allah!"[60]

Iʿtikāf - one of the important topics in Islamic Jurisprudence - has at times been the subject of independent writings. In the works of jurists such as al-Shāfiʿī and Abū Sulaymān Dāwūd al-Iṣfahānī, solitary writings under the title *Kitāb al-Iʿtikāf* can be found.[61]

---

[58] Shiʿrānī, Abūl Ḥasan, and Muḥammad Qarīb, *Nathr Ṭūbā ya Dāʾirat al-Maʿārif Lughāt al-Quran*, Pg. 181; Abīl Ḥusayn, Aḥmad ibn Fāris, *Muʿjam al-Maqāyīs fī al-Lughah*, Pg. 688; Rāghib al-Iṣfahānī, *Mufradāt Alfāẓ al-Quran.* Vol. 2, Pg. 632; Ṭurayḥī, Fakhr al-Dīn, *Majmaʿ al-Baḥrayn.* Vol. 3, Pg. 103; Ḥussayni, Sayyid Muḥammad, *Farhang Lughat va Estelāhāt Fiqhī*, Pg. 52.

[59] Hāshemī Shāhrūdī, Vol. 1, Pg 598; See also: Muḥaqqiq al-Ḥillī, *Sharāʾiʿ al-Islām fī Masāʾil al-Ḥalāl wa al-Ḥarām*, Vol. 1, Pg. 158; Shaykh al-Mufīd, Pg. 362; Rāghib al-Iṣfahānī, *Mufradāt Alfāẓ al-Quran*, Vol. 2, Pg. 632.

[60] Jurjānī, ʿAlī ibn Muḥammad, *Al-Taʿrifat*, Pg. 25.

[61] Ibn Nadīm, *Al-Fihrist*, Pp. 388, and 398.

Similarly, from the early Imāmī jurists, individuals such as Abūl Faḍl Ṣābūnī, Abū ʿAlī Askāfī, and Abū Jaʿfar ibn Mūsā ibn Bābawayh have written works entitled *Al-Iʿtikāf*.[62]

In Imāmī Jurisprudence of the middle and later periods, there are also some monographs on *iʿtikāf*, such as:

1. *Al-Iʿtikāfiyyah,* by Muʿīn al-Dīn Sālim ibn Badrān al-Baṣrī.
2. *Al-Iʿtikāfiyyah* or *Māʾ al-Ḥayāt wa Ṣāfī al-Furāt,* by Shaykh Luṭfullāh Mīsī al-Iṣfahānī.
3. *Al-Kifāf fī Masāʾil al-Iʿtikāf,* by Mullā Muḥammad Jaʿfar al-Sharīatmadārī.
4. *Al-Iʿtikāfiyyah,* by Sayyid Muḥammad ʿAlī al-Shahrestānī.[63]

History of Iʿtikāf

The history of *iʿtikāf* dates back to the time before the dawn of Islam, during the era of the past Prophets ﷺ and the Monotheists *(Muwaḥḥidīn)*.

At that time, *iʿtikāf* in the sense of the Islamic Jurisprudential term, along with its rules and conditions, was known simply as a form of devotion to the spirit of what *iʿtikāf* is today. Essentially, it involved going into spiritual seclusion and withdrawing from people for the purpose of self-discipline, contemplation, and introspection. However, even this form of spiritual retreat was present in some form among the past Prophets that Allah ﷻ sent for the guidance

[62] Najāshī, Abūl ʿAbbās, *Rijāl,* Pp. 359, 369, and 372.

[63] *Encyclopedia Islamica,* Vol. 9, Pg. 356.

of humanity.

As is evident from the tradition of the previous Prophets ﷺ, they frequently chose to seclude themselves during various times in their lives to seek proximity to Allah ﷻ, and to engage in self-purification, and strengthening of their souls. For extended periods of time and away from the materialistic world, they refrained from family life, and derived spiritual benefits from those periods of *iʿtikāf*.[64]

Thus, although Muslims adopted the practice of *iʿtikāf* from the tradition of Prophet Muḥammad ﷺ, similar practices existed in pre-Islamic religions, including among the Arabs.

There are reports suggesting that during the period of *Jāhiliyyah* (pre-Islamic Era of Ignorance), some individuals, such as the person who later became known as the second 'caliph' had made vows to perform *iʿtikāf* in Masjid al-Ḥarām (the Grand Masjid in Mecca), and later, at the dawn of Islam, Prophet Muḥammad ﷺ advised him to fulfill his vows of performing the *iʿtikāf*.[65]

Emphasis of the Prophet ﷺ on Iʿtikāf

The Prophet's ﷺ emphasis on *iʿtikāf* was to the extent that it became part of his annual practice.

Books of history recount that if any of his companions were not successful in performing *iʿtikāf*, they would make

[64] *Shīʿa Encyclopedia*, Vol. 2, Pg. 263.

[65] *Encyclopedia Islamica*, Vol. 9, Pg. 355.

up for it in the following year.[66]

In Medina, the Prophet ﷺ would engage in *i'tikāf* during the first ten days of the month of Ramaḍān in one year, then during the second ten days in the following year, and finally during the last ten days in the third year. For this purpose, a small tent or structure was set up for him in the Masjid.[67]

Moving to contemporary times, among the followers of the Ahlul Bayt, the tradition of *i'tikāf* - especially during the days of the 13th to the 15th of the month of Rajab - continues until today.

I'tikāf in the Life of the Immaculates

I'tikāf was also a matter of great significance for the Imams of the Ahlul Bayt. An example from the life of Imam Ḥusayn, reflects on the attention he gave to this spiritual retreat.

One day, a man came to see Imam Ḥasan ibn 'Alī, and said: "May my parents be sacrificed for you! Assist me in fulfilling a need."

Imam Ḥasan put on his shoes, stood up, and walked with the man towards Imam Ḥusayn, who was standing in the masjid, engaged in prayer.

He then turned to the man and asked: "Why did you not seek help from Ḥusayn, to fulfill your need?"

---

[66] Shahīd al-Thānī. *Al-Rawḍā al-Bahiyyah fī Sharḥ al-Lum'at al-Dimashqiyyah*, Vol. 1, Pg. 156.

[67] *Al-Kāfī*, Vol. 2, Pg. 175; Qummī, Shaykh 'Abbās al-. *Ṣafīnat al-Biḥār*, Vol. 3, Pg. 548.

The man replied: "I did, but he informed me that he was currently in *iʿtikāf* and unable to leave the masjid to attend to my need."[68]

Shīʿa Scholars and Iʿtikāf

A glance at the lives of the Shīʿa scholars reveals their commitment to this tradition of *iʿtikāf,* and how they made efforts not to let this beautiful tradition go to waste. In this respect, we share one story from a well-known scholar, Muqaddas Ardabīlī ﵀.[69]

During a year of famine and high prices of various commodities in the market, Muqaddas Ardabīlī ﵀ distributed all his food and groceries among the needy, taking only the share of a poor person for himself and his family. His wife, out of concern, objected and said: "Why do you deprive your own children and family of these necessities during these difficult times?"

---

68 *Al-Kāfī,* Vol. 4, Pg. 591.

69 Aḥmad ibn Muḥammad Ardabīlī (b. 908/1500, -d. 993/1585), also known as Muqaddas Ardabīlī and Muḥaqqiq Ardabīlī, was a Shīʿa jurist of the 10th/16th Century. He was a contemporary of Bahā' al-Dīn al-Āmilī, and he gained his fame from his asceticism and piety.

He was an expert in the Intellectual and Narrative Sciences, and assisted the Theological Seminary of Najaf to be more thriving for the time that he was its rector. One of his most important works was the book titled, *Zubdat al-Bayān fī Āyāt al-Aḥkām.*

He was so pious and ascetic that he became known as *"Muqaddas"* or "The Saintly or Sacred one." In addition, he was very humble towards his students, and there are countless stories narrated by them with respect to his humbleness and the help he provided to the needy.

Muqaddas Ardabīlī ﵀ said nothing, and as was his usual practice, went to the Grand Masjid of Kūfa for *iʿtikāf.* On the second day of his spiritual retreat, a man brought some flour and wheat to his house, telling his wife that it was sent by Muqaddas Ardabīlī ﵀ himself, who was currently in *iʿtikāf* at the Masjid of Kūfa.

Upon finishing his *iʿtikāf*, Muqaddas Ardabīlī ﵀ returned home, and when he learned about the incident, he thanked Allah ﷻ and realized that this blessing had come from Allah ﷻ, even though he had not been aware of it and had not instructed anyone to bring food to his house.[70]

Personal Effects and Blessings of Iʿtikāf

Creating a Conducive Environment for Contemplation

Concerns about making a living and the efforts to survive in life - especially in the present day when life has become challenging for people - have left no room for self-discovery, self-improvement, and contemplation. In this way, today's human beings have been deprived of this great act of worship: "Thinking, which is an act that, in itself, becomes the depth of other acts of worship, gives meaning and purpose to life, and plays the most significant role in achieving the secrets of existence, and reaching evolution and excellence."

Iʿtikāf provides the groundwork for this level of thinking.

During this period, daily work and routines are

---

[70] Mudarris Tabrīzī, Muḥammad ʿAlī, *Rayḥānat al-Adab*, Vol. 5, Pg. 368.

suspended, allowing a person's mind to be freed from many distractions and concerns.

As a result, the blessings of *i'tikāf* and adherence to its rules provide an opportunity for individuals to immerse themselves in profound thoughts, and through the practice of "thinking," achieve the marvels of thought. Following this, they can plan all their future activities based on this "thinking."

Let us not forget that the Noble Quran invites human beings to observe, pay attention, and contemplate on the world, essentially promoting practical thought, which begins with observation, gathering information, drawing conclusions, and then researching the correctness of these conclusions.

The Quran's emphasis on urging people to observe, pay attention, and contemplate served as a powerful incentive that led the Muslims of the past to pursue knowledge, science, and empirical research, sparking an intellectual movement in the Islamic society and the flourishing of knowledge and sciences among Muslims. This happened at a time when Europe was still in the darkness of ignorance.[71]

In this regard, Imam 'Alī ﷺ is quoted to have said: "Thinking will lead a person towards good deeds and encourage action upon them."[72]

He ﷺ also said: "Through thinking, the hidden affairs of

---

[71] Najātī, Muḥammad 'Uthmān, *Ḥadīth wa Rawān Shināsī*, Translation from Arabic to Farsi by Ḥamīd Riḍā Shaykhī.

[72] Faiḍ al-Kāshānī, Muḥsin. *Al-Maḥajjah al-Bayda fi Tahdhīb al-Ahyā'*, Vol. 8, Pg. 194.

existence become evident."[73]

The great mystic, Ibn Fanārī, writes: "The result of *iʿtikāf* is contemplation about matters that lead to union with the Lord. The outcome of contemplation in turn, is the remembrance of the Desired One, the Lord, and this remembrance of the Desired One takes place in His presence - on the sacred spiritual threshold."[74]

Historians have narrated a story about a person from Baṣra who went to see the mother of Abu Dharr al-Ghifārī to offer her condolences after Abu Dharr's death and asked her about his worship. In response, she simply replied: "I did not see much of his worship except that he would sit in a corner of the room during the day - deep in thought."[75]

An Opportunity for Asceticism

One of the blessings and positive outcomes of *iʿtikāf* is providing an opportunity for believers to engage in spiritual exercises.

Iʿtikāf keeps a person away from certain behaviours which the self takes pleasure in, such as using perfume, enjoying marital relations, and more. Instead, the spiritual retreat leads them to engage in fewer self-indulgent activities, such as fasting, which is a form of asceticism - that is, the practice of the denial of physical or psychological desires in order to

---

[73] Āmadī, ʿAbdul Wāḥid, *Ghurar al-Ḥikm wa Durar al-Kalim,* Vol. 3, Pg. 234, Ḥadīth 4322.

[74] Ibn Fanārī. *Miṣbāḥ al-Uns*, Pg. 56.

[75] *Al-Maḥajjah al-Bayda fi Tahdhīb al-Ahyāʾ*, Vol. 8. Pg. 194.

attain a spiritual ideal or goal.

From the perspective of mystics, it is impossible to achieve a successful spiritual journey without asceticism. Therefore, a person can only reach one's spiritual destination by accepting and engaging in asceticism - albeit for short spans of time, enduring the difficulties it entails, and gradually turning away from the pleasures that hinder one's spiritual progress.

Spiritual exercises are a significant tool for self-discipline because they help individuals moderate their desires, and gradually move away from excessive indulgence of the pleasures which this temporal world brings.

I'tikāf can serve as a starting point for spiritual self-discipline *(zuhd)*, or a valuable aid in establishing spiritual moderation practices which is one of the fundamental principles of spiritual progression. Since engaging in a life of *zuhd* is often less popular due to the difficulties it entails, individuals usually wait for an appropriate opportunity to start it. In this regard, *i'tikāf* provides one of the best opportunities to initiate such practices.

Mullā Ṣadrā ﵀, in discussing the importance of *zuhd*, writes: "The duty of a sincere wayfarer *(zāhid)*, and indeed the duty of one who has reached their spiritual destination, is to never refrain from practicing *zuhd*, self-struggle, and combat against the self throughout one's life, just as the Prophets ﵈, Imams ﵈, great mystics, and wise individuals conducted themselves. They never opened the doors to indulgence, or gluttony, and kept away from various types of fatty foods, sweet treats, drinks, etc., due to the blessings of gaining *zuhd* in their lives."[76]

قدر دل و پای جان یافتن   جز به ریاضت نتوان یافتن

سیم طبایع به ریاضت سپار   زر طبیعت به ریاضت برآر

تا ز ریاضت به مقامی رسی   کت به کسی درکشد این ناکسی

توسنی طبع چو رامت شود   سکه اخلاص به نامت شود

The value of the heart and soul's salvation,
Cannot be attained except through asceticism's foundation.

Like threading the silk of nature into asceticism's sphere,
And raising nature's gold through asceticism clear.

So that you reach a lofty station through your quest,
Whose peak no one else may attain, in earnest it's blessed.

For a temperance of nature brings your peace,
And an ascetic's pure coinage increase.[77]

Freedom from Scattered Thoughts and Attaining Inner Focus

One of the recommendations of the scholars of Islamic etiquette *(akhlāq)* and mysticism *('irfān)* is that the believers

[76] Mullā Ṣadrā, *Kasra Aḥkām al-Jāhiliyyah*, Pg. 104.
[77] Nezāmī Ganja'ī, *Kulliāt-e Khamsa*, Pg. 104.

need to ensure that they distance themselves from "scattered thoughts" and that they concentrate on reaching the stage of "inner focus."[78]

The term "scattered thoughts" which we are encouraged to remove from ourselves refers to the rejection, as much as possible, of one's imagination and the negative thoughts which it brings about. The term "inner focus" refers to the consolidation of one's positive thoughts, and overcoming their scattered and distracting nature so as to be able to focus and concentrate on Allah ﷻ and the religious teachings.

It is evident that as long as a person's thoughts are scattered, and one's heart does not find tranquility through inner focus, an individual will not be able to engage in contemplation, reach the Divine realm, or gain insight into hidden truths.

In the beautiful words of the famous poet, Rūmī:

جان همه روز از لگدکوب خیال　　وز زیان و سود وز بیم زوال

نی صفا می‌ماندش نی لطف و فر　　نی به سوی آسمان راه سفر

The soul's imagination is lost every day,
From loss and gain, from the fear of decline.

Neither purity remains, nor grace, nor nobility,
Nor is there a journey up to the Heavens.[79]

In order to practice liberation from mental scatteredness and

[78] Harawī Anṣārī, Khājeh ʿAbdullāh, *Rasāʾil Jāmiʿ*, Pg. 174.
[79] Mawlawī, *Mathnavī Maʿnavī.*

to be able to achieve inner concentration, there is no better time than the moments while one is engaged in *iʿtikāf.*

This narrow window of opportunity allows an individual to engage in serious contemplation for three days, effectively enabling them to navigate through the distractions, conflicts, and noises that surround them. During these moments of withdrawal from the hustle and bustle of social interactions, and the comings and goings of daily life, one can master their own thoughts and attain inner focus.

James S. Cutsinger[80] writes: "With a little effort, I can find a place of seclusion, however, closing my [material and spiritual] eyes is not an easy task. [Even when done], the images of the world still appear before my eyes like lightning, and the echoes of its sounds reverberate within me. Similarly, I can arrange daily retreats for myself and consider regular and consistent times for contemplation. I do not need to list for you the various myriad of matters that lead to mental scatteredness; you are aware of them yourself. Try dedicating your attention to just one thing for a few minutes, and you will immediately realize that the mind is like smoke, carried

---

[80] James S. Cutsinger, a respected religious studies professor, passed away on February 19, 2020, at the age of 66, after a battle with metastatic lung cancer. Born in 1953, he earned degrees in Political Theory and Theology, dedicating 38 years to teaching at the University of South Carolina. Known for his Socratic dialogue and "great books" classes, Cutsinger impacted many students and received accolades. As a scholar of the Perennial Philosophy, he focused on Frithjof Schuon's writings. A spiritual man, he found beauty in Eastern Orthodox traditions. Very devoted to his family, he embraced life with routine, humour, and a compassionate heart.

hither and thither by the wind. Do not forget that without inner focus - which is best practiced during moments of seclusion and distancing from people - you cannot attain the realm of tranquility derived from mastering the imagination."[81]

It is worth remembering that great Prophets like Mūsā ﷺ and Muḥammad ﷺ, upon receiving the gift of revelation and reaching the Divine realm, were able to gain control over their "imagination" by achieving inner focus through silence: the solitude on Mount Sinai *(Ṭūr al-Sinīn)* for Prophet Mūsā ﷺ, and the seclusion in the Cave of Ḥirā on the Mountain of Light *(Jabal al-Nūr)* for Prophet Muḥammad ﷺ are just two examples. Indeed, these great individuals viewed spiritual seclusion as a fundamental means for establishing a strong connection with Allah ﷻ, and the Nurturer also encouraged and urged them towards this practice.

The great scholars also discovered uncharted knowledge in moments of solitude and deep inner focus, making inventions and scientific discoveries.

Similarly, during moments of *iʿtikāf* and deep focus, the mystics of our faith tradition achieved spiritual insights, and during the times of "inner focus," they gained knowledge of hidden truths and mysteries.

Gaining control over one's desires is a challenge for many individuals, as they often believe they lack the ability to do so. Such individuals become discouraged when they hear talk about controlling the desires because they are unaware of their own potential for self-control. Thus, another blessing of

---

[81] Cutsinger, 1388: Pp. 270-271.

i'tikāf is that it practically informs individuals about their capability to control their desires and reminds them that, for at least three days, they can distance themselves from their desires - moderate them and manage them.

This reminder regarding one's ability to manage their material yearnings is embedded in the religious directive that states: "A person observing *i'tikāf* must abstain from sexual relations with their spouse, using perfume, eating, and drinking during the day - due to fasting being one of the necessary conditions of *i'tikāf* - and much more."[82] Certainly, someone who can control and moderate their desires for three days can manage them later on as well, and they may continue to succeed in this task for more extended periods in the future.

It is essential to remember that human desires are a Divine gift, as they are a source of nourishment and pleasure in this world. They ensure both enjoyment of life and the continuity of the human race, as people marry and benefit from the pleasures of having a spouse and through that union, children as well. Therefore, desires can be a source of blessings and contribute to the physical and spiritual development of one's life.

However, the point here is that these desires can only be beneficial for human beings when they are properly controlled. They contribute to the evolution of one's material and spiritual life, making existence in this world more

---

[82] *Taḥrīr al-Wasīlah*, Vol. 2, Pp. 48 and 49; *Sharā'i' al-Islām*. Vol. 1, Pg. 161; Shahīd al-Thānī, *Al-Rawḍā al-Bahiyyah fī Sharḥ al-Lum'at al-Dimashqiyyah*. Vol. 1, Pg. 158.

enjoyable when mastered and kept in balance, avoiding excesses. Otherwise, they can become a factor leading to the destruction of humanity, causing individuals to fall into various abnormalities and pitfalls.

Thus, by recalling an "individual's ability to control and moderate desires," *iʿtikāf* can serve as a starting point for managing instincts for those that do not believe that they have the inner ability to manage themselves, as they continuously suffer from the agony of excess in the life of this world.

Satisfying the Spiritual Needs

Usually, we experience various needs within ourselves, such as the need for clothing, food, water, recreation, support from others, and much more. Failing to meet these needs can expose a person to emotional distress and psychological disturbances.

Today, psychologists and mental health experts have accepted that meeting and satisfying human needs are effective for an individual's physical and mental well-being. Research has shown that if even one of an individual's basic needs is not met or is insufficiently fulfilled, then normal growth and mental well-being may become compromised. The role of fulfilling our needs is so fundamental to our existence that Maslow,[83] a famous psychologist, viewed

[83] Abraham Maslow (1908-1970) was an influential American psychologist best known for developing the Theory of Human

mental health as being attained through the satisfaction of basic human needs.[84]

However, human needs are not limited to the material and physical aspects. We have other needs as well, particularly those of a spiritual and emotional nature, such as the necessity for worshipping a higher Being - Allah, engaging in prayer, and engrossing ourselves in devotion to the Divine. In fact, the dual nature of the human being requires us to consider **both** of these dimensions of needs and to fulfill them both.

From this perspective, in addition to biological requirements, we also have unique needs known as 'spiritual needs.'[85]

Considering the above, another blessing of *i'tikāf* is its role in fulfilling a human being's spiritual necessities. In fact, *i'tikāf* serves as both a **symbol** and a rare **opportunity** for fulfilling these needs: it is a "symbol" because it can act as a successful experience for the person in *i'tikāf*, driving them towards any spiritual opportunity that can fulfill their spiritual and emotional needs; and it is also an "opportunity" itself, as it is a significant factor in satisfying the spiritual requirements of every individual.

Motivation and the Hierarchy of Needs, which has had a profound impact on the understanding of human behaviour and psychology.

[84] Sālārīfar, Muḥammad Riḍā, et al., *Behdāsht Ravānī bā Negārsh be Manābe' Islāmī*, Pg. 85.

[85] Ibid., Pg. 90.

An Opportunity for Improved Worship

Although, from an Islamic perspective, there are no restrictions on worshipping the Lord, and an individual can engage in supplication to one's Creator anytime and anywhere one's heart desires, there are certain times and places which are more suitable for worship. This is because in certain places and times, worship is more enjoyable, heartfelt, and closer to acceptance.

The late ʿAllāmah Ḥasanzādeh Āmulī[86] ﷺ puts this beautifully: "There is no doubt that the appropriateness of time is the most comprehensive appropriateness, just as being alive during the blessed month of Ramaḍān has a natural and creative effect on the hearts and souls."

The late Sayyid Ibn Ṭāwūs[87] ﷺ said: "Indeed, the times in

---

[86] The late ʿAllāmah Ḥasan Ḥasanzādeh Āmulī ﷺ was born on February 10, 1929, and passed away on September 25, 2021. He was a philosopher, mystic, theologian, scholar *(mujtahid)*, astronomer, and a teacher of religious and Islamic Seminary disciplines. ʿAllāmah Ḥasanzādeh ﷺ wrote many works regarding Jurisprudence, Philosophy, Ethics, Mysticism, Religious Wisdom, Theology, Mathematics, Astronomy, Arabic and Persian Literature, Natural Sciences, Ancient Medicine, and Occluded Sciences. However, most of his works are centered on the Quran, Philosophy, and Mysticism.

[87] Sayyid Raḍī al-Dīn ʿAlī ibn Mūsā ibn Jaʿfar ibn al-Ṭāwūs was born in 1193 CE and died in 1266 CE. He is famously known as Sayyid Ibn Ṭāwūs.

He was a great Shīʿa scholar, and authored numerous works, including the authoritative book on the Tragedy of Karbalāʾ known as *Al-Luhūf*, which is available in English, and many others.

the day and night in which the acceptance of Allah is present such that He would grant a person [through their acts of worship, spiritual openings], is kept a secret such that other than through Divine revelation, there is no other way to comprehend when it is."

Therefore, by providing an individual with a spiritually meaningful time and place which differs from many other times and places, *iʿtikāf* offers an opportunity for supplications to be answered. In addition, spiritual solitude derived from *iʿtikāf* is also another platform that a servant is blessed to reach - allowing for a more profound and deeper opportunity to pray to Allah ﷻ.

All people, to some extent, inevitably experience slips in life, however many of them - due to possessing an awakened conscience and innate spiritual inclinations - will eventually undergo the distressing feeling of being a "sinner."

Although the sense of feeling the "sin" after committing a wrong is beneficial and actually acts as a deterrent to future sins, preventing the repetition of sins and lapses, if it continues to remain within a person, then it will constantly subject them to the blows of reproach of the soul without

---

Due to his great ethical traits, piety, and constant attention to his deeds, spiritual experiences, and acts of wonder, he was famously known as *Jamāl al-ʿĀrifīn* - The Beauty of the Mystics. He was also called *Dhūl Ḥasbayn* - someone having two noble sides of birth - because on the one hand, his lineage reached Imam Ḥasan al-Mujtabā ﵇, and on the other hand, his great grandfather was Dāwūd ibn Ḥasan al-Muthanna, the grandson of Imam al-Sajjād's ﵇ daughter - and thus a descendant of Imam al-Ḥusayn ﵇.

offering a seasoning of hope. This 'beneficial force' can actually transform itself into becoming an inhibiting factor on the path of one's spiritual growth.

Allah ﷻ therefore, has provided His servants with the support of hope in the form of repentance *(tawbah)*, so that by relying on the ability to turn back to Him, they can remain safe from the aforementioned detrimental consequences of sinning, and can consistently stay on the path of spiritual development and devout elevation.

The Noble Quran illustrates the method of repentance as a unique and effective way to address the feeling of sin - because repentance or returning back to Allah ﷻ - leads to the forgiveness of sins, strengthens human hope for gaining Divine satisfaction, and reduces anxiety and spiritual agitation.

Furthermore, true repentance often encourages an individual to improve and self-rectify, making them ready to avoid falling into the trap of sins and mistakes over again. The act of seeking repentance also helps an individual understand one's self-worth and increase self-confidence and satisfaction with Allah ﷻ and oneself, thus stabilizing one's own sense of security and mental peace.[88]

I'tikāf is one of those times when the hope of the acceptance of repentance from Allah ﷻ is more than many other times, thus, a person can have a higher degree of confidence in the acceptance of their asking forgiveness, and it being accepted by Allah ﷻ.

Such hope and confidence will play a significant role in

---

[88] *Ḥadīth wa Rawān Shināsī*, Pg. 411.

rescuing an individual from the distressing sense of sin, followed by anxiety and restlessness, born out of this sense of breaking the laws of Almighty Allah ﷻ.

An Opportunity to Satisfy the Need for "Solitude"

Sometimes, a person yearns to be alone, completely isolated from everyone. In these moments of solitude, the individual may need to withdraw from their closest friends and may even find it unbearable to be around their dearest loved ones, seeking to be alone with their own thoughts and reflections.

This inner desire, especially in an era of industry and technology - an era characterized by the iron and concrete jungles we live in, the excessive levels of pollution, and the uncontrolled environmental degradation, where people are often lacking in emotions and affection for one another - is felt more intensely.

Iʿtikāf provides an excellent opportunity to fulfill this inner need of seclusion, allowing a person to momentarily set aside the discomforts caused by the lack of sociability and compassion, and enables an individual to find oneself by distancing from everyone and everything. This way, one can better explore the hidden aspects of one's inner self.

An Exercise in the Liberation from Media Dependency

The entry of various forms of media into people's lives and the influence which it wields on individuals has given rise to "media dependency," with many people spending an extensive amount of time on a daily basis "entertaining" themselves with media on their televisions, computer screens, tablets, and more often than not, their mobile phones.

Nowadays, this dependency has become so severe that more and more people are, for various reasons, becoming depressed, despondent, and agitated if they are forced to distance themselves from media consumption for even a few minutes.

It seems as though people have become **addicted** to the consumption of media - just as someone addicted to drugs is always looking for their next fix; or how an alcoholic cannot live without imbibing another drink.

The essence of this behaviour is media dependence and the dominance of media over individuals - to the point that most of the time, the primary use of media is for leisure and entertainment, rather than necessity and justifiable uses.

The nights and days of *i'tikāf* provide an excellent opportunity to create balance in media consumption and the ability to liberate oneself from its dominance, provided that the individual abstains from having their devices, or turns off their phone and all other gadgets during these few days.

This experience helps them resist the influence of media, and instead of being **controlled by it**, they actually gain **control over it**. Through such mastery, in their ongoing life, they will be able to make choices with determination, and use their technology more responsibly, and will be careful about what types of media they consume and what they refrain from - and how much.

Social Blessings of Iʿtikāf

The social blessings of *iʿtikāf* should be sought within the Jurisprudential teachings of this act of spiritual seclusion. The teachings are structured in such a way that, in addition to ensuring the validity of *iʿtikāf*, they also bring about order and improvement to a person's social relationships. By adhering to these teachings, a person can establish their social relationships in accordance with Islamic principles, and the invaluable guidance given by Prophet Muḥammad ﷺ and his Ahlul Bayt ﷺ.

Freedom from Contention and Dispute

One of the social benefits of *iʿtikāf* is the refinement of one's speech, which includes refraining from engaging in disputes and arguments with others. This concept is derived from a Jurisprudential ruling which states: "Engaging in disputes or arguments, whether of a worldly or religious nature, to prevail over the opposing party, or to assert superiority, is prohibited for a person during *iʿtikāf*."[89]

In essence, it reflects a need for Muslims to realize that they must always rely on logical discourses and avoid trying to compel the other person to accept their words without thought and serious reflection.

Islam advises its followers to engage in logical and evidence-based dialogue, while emphasizing the avoidance of dispute, without requiring the individual to seek validation and confirmation of their words from others.

---

[89] *Farhang-e-Fiqh.* Vol. 1, Pg. 600.

This Islamic approach, meaning refraining from argumentation and avoiding the act of trying to coerce the opposing party into accepting one's own words - an essential element of any argument - not only aids the principle of "freedom in accepting perspectives," but it also eliminates the grounds for self-centeredness of an individual. It serves as one of the fundamental mechanisms to prevent conflicts and resentment and can help in preserving love and sincerity among individuals.

From this perspective, one of the social effects of the spiritual retreat - resulting from the prohibition of a person in *iʿtikāf* engaging in any sort of argumentation - is the avoidance of divisive factors, and the preservation of love and decorum among people.

There is an event that took place during the time of Prophet Muḥammad ﷺ in which a group of his companions are quoted to have said: "The Messenger of Allah came out to us one day while we were disputing something related to the matters of religion. He became extremely angry, such that we had never seen him so angry before. Then he said: 'Indeed, those who came before you were destroyed because of this (disputing). Avoid disputes, for a believer does not indulge in disputes. Avoid disputes, for verily, one who indulges in disputes has incurred a great loss. Avoid disputes, for on the Day of Judgement, I will not intercede for the one who indulged in disputes. Avoid disputes, for I am the leader of three categories in Paradise - its outskirts, its middle, and its highest parts - for the one who abandons disputing while being truthful. Avoid disputes, for the first thing my Lord prohibited me from - after worshipping idols - was disputing.'"[90]

Assistance and Relief for Others

Iʿtikāf teaches us to step outside the realm of self-absorption and be considerate of the thoughts and needs of others. It encourages us - to the extent possible - to help untie the knots in the lives of other people - most notably those who are going through unbearable difficulties.

When a person in *iʿtikāf* becomes aware of the religious decree that states: "It is not permissible for someone in a state of *iʿtikāf* to leave the masjid unless it becomes absolutely necessary, such as when one wants to fulfill the need of a fellow believer; and in this case, leaving the masjid is allowed,"[91] they learn the importance of helping others and striving to fulfill the needs of fellow believers. This, to the extent that it makes leaving the masjid during *iʿtikāf* - which is normally an unlawful act - become permissible. The

---

[90] *Biḥār al-Anwār*, Vol. 2, Pg. 138:
وَرُوِيَ عَنْ أَبِي الدَّرْدَاءِ وَأَبِي أُمَامَةَ وَوَاثِلَةَ وَأَنَسٍ قَالُوا: خَرَجَ عَلَيْنَا رَسُولُ اللّٰهِ ﷺ يَوْمًا وَنَحْنُ نَتَمَارَى فِي شَيْءٍ مِنْ أَمْرِ الدِّينِ فَغَضِبَ غَضَبًا شَدِيدًا لَمْ يَغْضَبْ مِثْلَهُ ثُمَّ قَالَ: إِنَّمَا هَلَكَ مَنْ كَانَ قَبْلَكُمْ بِهٰذَا ذَرُوا الْمِرَاءَ فَإِنَّ الْمُؤْمِنَ لَا يُمَارِي ذَرُوا الْمِرَاءَ فَإِنَ الْمُمَارِيَ قَدْ تَمَّتْ خَسَارَتُهُ ذَرُوا الْمِرَاءَ فَإِنَّ الْمُمَارِيَ لَا أَشْفَعُ لَهُ يَوْمَ الْقِيَامَةِ ذَرُوا الْمِرَاءَ فَأَنَا زَعِيمٌ بِثَلَاثَةِ أَبْيَاتٍ فِي الْجَنَّةِ فِي رِيَاضِهَا وَأَوْسَطِهَا وَأَعْلَاهَا لِمَنْ تَرَكَ الْمِرَاءَ وَهُوَ صَادِقٌ ذَرُوا الْمِرَاءَ فَإِنَّ أَوَّلَ مَا نَهَانِي عَنْهُ رَبِّي بَعْدَ عِبَادَةِ الْأَوْثَانِ الْمِرَاءُ.

[91] Najafī, Muḥammad Ḥasan, *Jawāhir al-Kalām fī Sharḥ Sharāʾiʿ al-Islam*, Vol. 17, Pg. 182; *Farhang-e-Fiqh*, Vol. 1, Pg. 599.

essence of this statement is for an individual to prioritize moments of helping others - over moments of *iʿtikāf* which is helping oneself.

Imam Jaʿfar al-Ṣādiq ﷺ said: "Whoever strives to fulfill the need of a fellow believer, and Allah grants them that need, the Almighty will record for them one *ḥajj*, one *ʿumrah*, and a two-month *iʿtikāf* in Masjid al-Ḥarām, along with fasting during that time. If despite their efforts, one fails to fulfill the fellow believer's need, then Allah will (still) record for them one *ḥajj* and one *ʿumrah*."[92]

تا توانی اگر از غم دگران برهانی — به ز صد ناقه حمراست به قربان بردن

بردن غم ز دل خسته دلی در میزان — به ز صوم رمضان است به شعبان بردن

به ز آزادی صد بنده فرمان بردار — حاجت مؤمن محتاج به احسان بردن

دست افتاده بگیری ز زمین برخیزد — به ز شبخیزی و شاباش زیاران بردن

As long as you have the ability, strive to help others to relieve their sorrows,

---

[92] *Al-Kāfī*, Vol. 4, Pg. 589:

عَنْ أَبِي عَبْدِ اللهِ عليه السلام قَالَ: مَنْ سَعَى فِي حَاجَةِ أَخِيهِ الْمُسْلِمِ فَاجْتَهَدَ فِيهَا فَأَجْرَى اللهُ عَلَىٰ يَدَيْهِ قَضَاءَهَا كَتَبَ اللهُ عَزَّ وَجَلَّ لَهُ حَجَّةً وَعُمْرَةً وَاعْتِكَاف شَهْرَيْنِ فِي الْمَسْجِدِ الْحَرَامِ وَصِيَامَهُمَا وَإِنِ اجْتَهَدَ فِيهَا وَلَمْ يُجْرِ اللهُ قَضَاءَهَا عَلَىٰ يَدَيْهِ كَتَبَ اللهُ عَزَّ وَجَلَّ لَهُ حَجَّةً وَ عُمْرَةً.

Even if that means offering one hundred red camels in sacrifice.

Relieving grief from a weary heart is a weighty act,
Similar to preparing to fast the month of Ramaḍān, and performing good acts in the month of Shaʿbān.

Take charge and receive the rewards of the emancipation of one hundred slaves,

And fulfill the need of even one believer through your benevolence.

If you grasp the fallen hand, it may rise from the ground,

And celebrate through the night vigil, and the morning cheer with comrades abound.[93]

Compassion for Others

When a person, for whatever reason, cannot help to alleviate the difficulties of someone or fulfill their needs, then "compassion" is a great substitute.

Compassion for the deprivation, pain and sufferings of others is the smallest level of feeling empathy towards one's fellow human beings. If a person reaches this level, then it fulfills the meaning of Saʿdī's famous line of poetry:

تو کز محنت دیگران بی غمی   نشاید که نامت نهند آدمی

You who are indifferent to other peoples' misfortunes,

---

[93] *Al-Maḥajjah al-Bayḍā' fi Tahdhīb al-Ahyā'*, Pg. 315.

Do not expect the title of 'human' for your portion.[94]

Compassion involves considering others, granting them dignity, and becoming a partner in their sorrows. Those who lack even this minimal level of empathy are at risk of drowning in self-centeredness and indifference.

Furthermore, unconcern and apathy towards the suffering of others can potentially lead a person to a fate similar to those who are currently suffering, due to the laws of cause and effect that govern human society.

Just as our entire body's reaction to phenomena like fire, needles, and pain signifies the proper functioning of that body, if our soul does not react to the pain and suffering of others, then it signals a disorder or illness in the spiritual heart. This is because we are all part of human society - and the sign of a healthy member is restlessness, unease, and sorrow when another member is suffering.

Seclusion in *iʿtikāf* guides a person to have "compassion" towards others as another one of its social benefits.

"Compassion" with fellow human beings through the spiritual seclusion is emphasized by the necessity of fasting for a person in the retreat, since "one of the conditions for the validity of *iʿtikāf* is fasting, and without fasting, the *iʿtikāf* is not valid."[95]

Fasting leads individuals who do not experience hunger throughout the year - due to financial comforts - to **have** to feel it during the days of fasting. This helps them remember

---

[94] Saʿdī, Abū Muḥammad Muṣliḥ al-Dīn, *Gulistān*, Section One on the Methodologies of the Kings, Wisdom 10, Line 10.

[95] *Taḥrīr al-Wasīlah*, Vol. 2, Pg. 42; *Sharāʾiʿ al-Islām*, Vol. 1, Pg. 160.

the plight of the poor and practically empathize with them.

This, on one hand, contributes to the mental well-being of an individual; and on the other hand, promotes the mental health of the community as well.

The wealthy, by gaining this internal experience upon completion of the *iʿtikāf*, should feel empathy for others and generously contribute from their own wealth that they have been blessed with. This act will lead to their inner purification from miserliness and other spiritual abnormalities.

On the other hand, the needy in society, as a result of these empathetic contributions will achieve relative prosperity, undoubtedly ensuring the alleviation of poverty in society, and consequently, an improvement in living standards - guaranteeing better mental health of the community.[96]

Visiting the Sick and Showing Compassion

In the religious jurisprudence of *iʿtikāf*, it is stated: "A person in *iʿtikāf* cannot leave the masjid, except for a necessity like visiting the sick."[97]

This religious rule instructs a person in *iʿtikāf* about yet another social duty, which is taking care of the sick and visiting them. It conveys to the believers that visiting the sick, as a social responsibility, can take precedence over hours spent in *iʿtikāf*, and can even bring about a higher reward.

---

[96] *Behdāsht Ravānī bā Negārsh be Manābe' Islāmī*, Pg. 200.

[97] *Sharāʾiʿ al-Islām*, Vol. 1, 160; Narāqī, Aḥmad, *Mustanad al-Shīʿa ilā Aḥkām al-Sharīʿah*. Vol. 10, Pg. 560.

This rule encourages a person in *iʿtikāf* to prioritize caring for the sick who need attention, over the time spent in seclusion with Allah ﷻ.

Visiting the sick has several benefits:

1. It provides comfort and strengthens the heart of an ill person.
2. It accelerates their recovery process.
3. It increases their resilience against an illness.
4. It fosters hope in them for continued life.
5. It helps prevent them from feeling like a burden on society.
6. It promotes gratitude in the person visiting the patient for one's own health.
7. It motivates the patient to make the most of their health.

These wisdoms inherent in visiting the sick can be the key to choosing to visit a sick patient to staying in *iʿtikāf* in a masjid. In this regard, Prophet Muḥammad ﷺ said: "Whoever enquires about the condition of a sick person and visits them, at that moment, it is as if they are sitting in the orchard of the fruit-trees of Paradise. When they get up, 70,000 angels will be their guards and will supplicate for them until the evening."[98]

Prophet Muḥammad ﷺ also said: "When someone visits a sick person, they become a recipient of the Mercy of Allah."[99]

---

[98] Ghazālī, *Iḥyāʾ al-ʿUlūm al-Dīn*, Vol. 2, Pg. 451.
[99] Ibid.

Showing Respect for the Deceased

Another social benefit which is derived from *iʿtikāf* is that it reminds a person to respect one's fellow Muslims - even those who are deceased.

It teaches a person that during *iʿtikāf*, one is not allowed to leave the masjid except for purposes which Islam has deemed to be more important than the spiritual state that one is seeking to develop in the masjid - one of them being accompanying a funeral procession of a fellow believer.[100] This act bestows dignity upon the departed soul, brings solace to their spirit, and provides comfort to the surviving loved ones. Taking part in a funeral serves as a source of admonition and reflection for those who are accompanying the deceased to the graveyard, leading to moderation in the desires and worldly pursuits of the mourner.

In accordance with the law of 'action' and 'reaction,' it prompts others to also behave respectfully and with dignity, meaning that they too learn how to conduct themselves with due decorum during the funeral procession.

Prophet Muḥammad ﷺ is quoted as having said: "Participate in funeral processions, for it will remind you of the Hereafter."[101]

The 8th Imam, ʿAlī ibn Mūsā al-Riḍā (ʿa) said: "Whoever accompanies a funeral procession of one of our friends (a *Shīʿa)*, all their sins will be forgiven, and they will be just as they were on the day they were born (sinless)."[102]

---

[100] *Sharāʾiʿ al-Islām*, Vol. 1, Pg. 160; *Taḥrīr al-Wasīlah*, Vol. 2, Pg. 46.

[101] *Ṣafīnat al-Biḥār*, Vol. 2, Pg. 924.

[102] Ibid., Pg. 925.

Family Building and Preservation

Sometimes the zeal for worship can distract a person from more critical matters, and can lead to neglecting the rights of others, or even disrupting relationships. Therefore, the Jurisprudential rulings regarding acts of worship are designed to ensure that a person does not remain deficient in more crucial matters, or in cases of an apparent conflict between worship and something more important, to allow a person to choose the more important matter.

For example, in one of the Jurisprudential rulings related to *iʿtikāf*, it is stated that: "One of the conditions for the validity of *iʿtikāf* is that a wife requires the permission of her husband."[103]

This Jurisprudential ruling serves as a reminder about the importance of family foundations and places the superiority of that over any form of recommended worship, including *iʿtikāf*, which could potentially harm those foundations.

In essence, a person, in this case a wife, who is engaging in *iʿtikāf* learns that Allah ﷻ has made His satisfaction conditional upon the satisfaction of her spouse through this ruling.

With this decree, Allah ﷻ closes the path to marital discord, and reminds couples about the importance of mutual satisfaction in the course of life. It underscores the significance of ensuring that the value of kindness prevails in the family environment and steers a couple towards family-

---

[103] *Sharāʾiʿ al-Islām*, Vol. 1, Pg. 159; *Taḥrīr al-Wasīlah*, Vol. 2: Pg. 44; *Farhang-e-Fiqh*. Vol. 1, Pg. 599.

centeredness and the preservation of the rights of one another.

Respecting the Sanctity of One's Parents

Respecting the sanctity of one's parents is another lesson that *iʿtikāf* reminds a person of, and in this way, an individual benefits from another social blessing of the spiritual seclusion.

This teaching is derived from the following legal ruling which states: "Another condition for the validity of *iʿtikāf* is that if a child's spiritual seclusion causes distress to one's parents, then the child must obtain explicit permission from their parents."[104]

Based on this ruling, a person learns that *iʿtikāf* accompanied by causing distress to one's parents and not obtaining their consent is not valid or correct from the outset.

In fact, to understand the lofty position of parents and the necessity of respecting them, there is actually no need even to refer to verses of the Quran and the narrations *(aḥādīth)* of Prophet Muḥammad ﷺ and his Ahlul Bayt ﵈! Rather, it is sufficient for an individual to turn to one's conscience and recognize that they are morally obligated to appreciate those people who laboured for years and years, endured pain and hardship, and suffered immensely for them - and who can that be other than one's parents?!

There is also an imperative within Islam that we must refrain from insulting and disrespecting those who are older

---

[104] *Taḥrīr al-Wasīlah,* Vol. 2, Pg. 44; *Farhang-e-Fiqh,* Vol. 1, Pg. 599.

than us, and merely because of them being older, they have extensive rights over us who are younger than them!

It is natural for a conscientious person at such times - guided by the dictates of reason and conscience - never to act unjustly towards one's parents and always strive to uphold their sanctity and rights.

Respecting Others

Iʿtikāf may be vulnerable to "abuse," just like any other act of worship. Therefore, it is essential to be vigilant so that this important and impactful act of worship does not become subject to such harm. Otherwise, its performance in society and its over-all effectiveness on the soul of an individual may decrease, and it might even shift from being a spiritual act of devotion to Allah ﷻ to a mere means of passing time, and simply another personal activity devoid of its true essence and nature.

In the following section, we will discuss some potential issues that can threaten the practice of *iʿtikāf*, recognizing that neglecting them can disrupt this elevated form of worship:

1. One of the things which can affect the benefits of *iʿtikāf* is the presence of mobile phones. The phenomenon of carrying and using these devices contradicts the essence of seclusion, which is meant to be moments of spiritual solitude, worship, and profound contemplation. As such, mobile phones and other such devices can significantly undermine the effectiveness of *iʿtikāf*. Moreover, the interference they cause is not limited to the owner of the mobile phone, but

rather, the ringing of the phone at all hours and conversations can cause disruption and distraction for others as well, hindering their focused presence of mind. Of course, if a person keeps their phone with them to use Islamically-themed apps such as the Quran, supplications, or Islamic books to read to better themselves, then this is not a problem. The concern, however, is that there may always be a desire to check messages or respond to emails if one has their phone or any other devices with them.

2. Another issue is the presence of individuals who may come into the masjid for filming or interviewing those in *iʿtikāf* to use as promotional material for the community.

This can distract the *iʿtikāf* participants and engage their minds in appearing and looking attractive for the camera. Moreover, some people might feel the desire to be selected for an interview which can then lead to disappointment if they are not chosen, and cause them to lose focus, or even become jealous for why others were chosen over them.

On the other hand, if they are chosen, they might become subjects of pride or ostentation, or may end up spending their time reviewing what they will say during the interview, or going over what they should have said after it - fearing that they may have made a mistake or not appeared as appealing or charming as they would have liked. This can detract them from the spiritual experience of *iʿtikāf* and its countless blessings.

3. Another issue is placing excessive importance on *ifṭār* - the food eaten to break the fast, as well as *suḥūr* - the pre-dawn meal during the three days of *iʿtikāf,* and enjoying delicious, fatty, or sweet dishes for these meals.

Proper nutrition and attention to the quality and quantity of food are very important so that the believer has the physical and mental strength to fast and engage in worship over the period of the *iʿtikāf*. However, we must not forget that one of the primary purposes of *iʿtikāf* is self-discipline and controlling ourselves and taming the sin of gluttony. Therefore, overly focusing on food and complaining about potential shortcomings in the meals has no real connection with the spiritual essence of *iʿtikāf and* can lead participants away from the true goals of this practice.

4. Many times, the masājid chosen for *iʿtikāf* are located in residential areas, and this can create disturbances for the neighbours. These disturbances might include participants being too loud, an excess amount of traffic to and from the masjid, and other such noises. It is essential to manage these three days in a way that ensures no inconvenience to neighbours and keeps the sacred space of *iʿtikāf* free from any sounds that might cause distress to the local community.

In summary, these are important aspects to consider during *iʿtikāf* to maintain the true spiritual essence of this practice and avoid distractions or disruptions that may arise during these days of devotion and self-reflection.

May Allah ﷻ allow us all to partake in *iʿtikāf* at least once in our lifetime, and may it be a means to transform ourselves into the spiritual beings we were destined to be.

The Virtues of Iʿtikāf and Islamic Rulings[105]

Iʿtikāf is a virtuous act of worship *(ʿibādah)*, which entails residing for a set number of days and nights in a masjid, while being in the state of fasting. Performing *iʿtikāf* in the months of Rajab and Ramaḍān is highly advantageous.

It is narrated that Imam Jaʿfar al-Ṣādiq said: "Whenever the last ten days of the month of Ramaḍān would come, the Prophet of Allah would retreat to the masjid, and they [the companions] would set up a tent for him made of the hide of an animal, then he would roll up the skirting and lay out his bedding."[106]

Imam al-Ṣādiq has also been quoted as saying: "The Battle of Badr took place in the month of Ramaḍān, so the Prophet was not able to partake in *iʿtikāf* that year; but

---

[105] From this point onward until the end of this book, we present the rulings of *iʿtikāf* as presented by Āyatullāh Sayyid ʿAlī al-Ḥusaynī al-Sīstānī.

[106] *Wasāʾil al-Shīʿa*, Vol. 10, *Kitāb al-Iʿtikāf*, Chapter 1, Pg. 533, Ḥadīth 1:

كَانَ رَسُولُ اللهِ إِذَا كَانَ الْعَشْرُ الْأَوَاخِرُ اعْتَكَفَ فِي الْمَسْجِدِ وَضُرِبَتْ لَهُ قُبَّةٌ مِنْ شَعْرٍ وَشَمَّرَ الْمِئْزَرَ وَطَوَى فِرَاشَهُ.

instead, he engaged in *iʿtikāf* twice [back to back in the month of Ramaḍān] the following year: ten days for that current year, and ten days in compensation for the previous year [of having missed out]."[107]

In a final narration which we quote from Imam al-Ṣādiq ﷺ, it is noted that Prophet Muḥammad ﷺ said: "The rewards of engaging in *iʿtikāf* for ten days during the month of Ramaḍān are equivalent to the performance of two *ḥajj* and two *ʿumrah*."[108]

Iʿtikāf was a custom of Prophet Muḥammad ﷺ which Muslims are also encouraged to perform, and it is an act of worship that has been mentioned in some of the past Divinely-sent teachings as well, although there are differences in the details and specifics [as to how past nations performed their *iʿtikāf*]. However, this indicates the importance of this act of worship, just as Allah ﷻ says in the Noble Quran:

﴿وَإِذْ جَعَلْنَا ٱلْبَيْتَ مَثَابَةً لِّلنَّاسِ وَأَمْنًا وَٱتَّخِذُوا۟ مِن مَّقَامِ إِبْرَٰهِـۧمَ مُصَلًّى ۖ وَعَهِدْنَآ إِلَىٰٓ إِبْرَٰهِـۧمَ وَإِسْمَـٰعِيلَ أَن طَهِّرَا بَيْتِىَ لِلطَّآئِفِينَ وَٱلْعَـٰكِفِينَ وَٱلرُّكَّعِ ٱلسُّجُودِ ﴿١٢٥﴾﴾

And remember when We made the House [the

---

[107] *Kitab al-Iʿtikāf*, Chapter 1, Pg. 533, Ḥadīth 2:
كَانَتْ بَدْرٌ فِي شَهْرِ رَمَضَانَ فَلَمْ يَعْتَكِفْ رَسُولُ اللهِ فَلَمَّا أَنْ كَانَ مِنْ قَابِلٍ اعْتَكَفَ رَسُولُ اللهِ عِشْرِينَ عَشْرًا لِعَامِهِ وَعَشْرًا قَضَاءً لِمَا فَاتَهُ.

[108] *Wasāʾil al-Shīʿa*, Pg. 534, Ḥadīth 3:
قَالَ رَسُولُ اللهِ ﷺ: إِعْتِكَافُ عَشْرٍ فِي شَهْرِ رَمَضَانَ تَعْدِلُ حَجَّتَيْنِ وَعُمْرَتَيْنِ.

> Kaʿbah in Mecca] a place of return for the people, and [a refuge of safety, a sanctuary, that is, a sign of the truth]. And (We said): stand in prayer [O believers, as you did in earlier times] in the Station of Ibrāhīm *(Maqām-e-Ibrāhīm)*. And We imposed a duty on Ibrāhīm and Ismāʾīl [saying]: 'Purify My House for those who go around it as a rite of worship, and those who abide in devotion *(iʿtikāf)*, and those who bow down and prostrate [in the prayer].'"[109]

To escape from the passions of the soul, and to flee from worldly occupations and develop a deeper relationship with Allah ﷻ, believers need solitude in order to wash themselves from the rust of sins, and be able to whole-heartedly repent, and engage in self-purification.

Iʿtikāf provides the grounds for such an opportunity.

By taking refuge in a masjid, fasting, and avoiding worldly affairs or distractions, the act of *iʿtikāf* opens the way to spiritual evolution, and provides the means for a person's repentance to be accepted by Allah ﷻ, and for them to achieve many Divine rewards.

---

[109] Quran, Sūrah al-Baqarah (2), Verse 125.

Meaning of I'tikāf and Its Duration

Issue 1: *I'tikāf*, according to the legal definition *(sharī'ah)* means that a person stays in a masjid [for a set number of days] with the intention of attaining spiritual proximity to Allah ﷻ. According to recommended precaution *(iḥtiyāṭ mustaḥabb)*, an individual needs to stay inside the masjid with the intention of performing acts of worship, such as prayers *(ṣalāt)*, supplications *(du'ā')*, or the like.

I'tikāf is one of the recommended *(mustaḥabb)* acts of worship that can become obligatory *(wājib)* through certain things, such as a pledge to Allah ﷻ *(nadhr)*, a promise to Allah ﷻ *(qasam)*, and the like.

Issue 2: *I'tikāf* does not have a specific time when it should be performed, thus it can be done any time during the year when fasting is permissible [any month of the year, other than those days such as the two days of *'Eid* when it is not permissible to fast]; however, the best time for it is in the blessed month of Ramaḍān, and within that month, the best time is during the last ten days of the month.

Issue 3: The minimum amount of time which one can perform the *i'tikāf* is three days along with the two nights in the middle of those three days, and anything less than that is not permissible. However, it is permissible to engage in *iʿtikāf* for more than three days, even if it is a greater amount - such as a day or a night more, or even a part of a day or a night more (than the necessary three days).[110]

DAY 1	NIGHT 1	DAY 2	NIGHT 2	DAY 3
Iʿtikāf starts with the *adhān* of *Fajr*	*Iʿtikāf*	*Iʿtikāf*	*Iʿtikāf*	*Iʿtikāf* ends with the *adhān* of *Maghrib*

It is worth mentioning that *iʿtikāf* does not have a maximum number of days. However, if a person spends five full days in this spiritual retreat, then they must also stay in the *iʿtikāf* for the sixth day as well. In fact, according to obligatory precaution *(iḥtiyāṭ wājib)*, whenever a person adds two days to one's *iʿtikāf*, then the obligatory precaution is to stay the next day as well (such that it becomes multiples of three days). Therefore, if an individual remains in the state of *iʿtikāf* for eight days, then it is obligatory to observe *iʿtikāf* on the ninth day as well; and the same is true for the twelfth and fifteenth days, etc.

Issue 4: The beginning of the calculation for the three days -

---

[110] Therefore, there is no obstacle to include the first or fourth night in the intention of *iʿtikāf* so one can go to the masjid a bit earlier in the night and stay a bit extra after the completion of the three days.

which is the minimum time for *iʿtikāf* - is the [start of or just before the] morning *(Fajr)* call to prayer *(adhān)* on the first day; and the end of the period of *iʿtikāf* will be the evening *(Maghrib)* call to prayer on the third day, according to obligatory precaution.[111]

This means that a person cannot initiate *iʿtikāf* **after** the morning call to prayer on the first day, even if they make up for the lack of starting on the first day [before the *adhān* of *Fajr*] by staying an extra day on the fourth day.

For example, staying in the masjid from the noon *(Ẓuhr)* call to prayer on the first day to the noon call to prayer on the fourth day [would not be sufficient, and such an *iʿtikāf* will be invalid].

---

[111] Of course, a person can have the intention of *iʿtikāf* on the first night (before the morning call to prayer on the first day) and the fourth night (after the evening call to prayer on the third day), however, this period will be not counted as part of the actual three days in the calculation.

Conditions for a Correct Iʿtikāf

For *iʿtikāf* to be valid, it must meet the following conditions:

First to Fourth Condition

1. The person performing it must be a Muslim.
2. The person must be sane.
3. The person must perform *iʿtikāf* with the intention of seeking proximity to Allah ﷻ.
4. The person must perform *iʿtikāf* for a minimum of three days [and two nights].

Issue 5: A person who does *iʿtikāf* [the Islamic term for this person is that they are a *muʿtakif*] must be a Muslim, and of sound mind (not mentally unstable); however, maturity (being *bāligh*) is not a condition, and thus *iʿtikāf* of a young child who is regarded as *mumayyiz*[112] is also valid.

Also, it is necessary for the *muʿtakif* that from the beginning to the end of the *iʿtikāf*, as mentioned in the first volume [of our Islamic Laws manual] under the topic of the

---

112 *Mumayyiz*: The age at which a child can discern between right and wrong, and (the age at which) he or she knows about the differences between a man and a woman.

intention of the ablution *(wuḍū)*,[113] to have the intention of seeking closeness to Allah ﷻ and engaging in this act as a demonstration of pure sincerity *(ikhlāṣ)* towards Allah ﷻ. Also, as mentioned in **Issue 3** (of this book), it is necessary to partake in *iʿtikāf* for at least three days.

Fifth Condition

5. The person must be in the state of fasting [during the daytime - just as one would do during the month of Ramaḍān].

Issue 6: The *muʿtakif* must fast during the days of *iʿtikāf*. Therefore, *iʿtikāf* of a person who cannot fast, such as a sick person, a woman in her monthly cycle *(ḥayḍ)*, or a woman who is bleeding from child delivery *(nifās)*, is not valid.

Of course, fasting during the days of *iʿtikāf* does not have

---

[113] This is in reference to the first volume of the *Comprehensive Islamic Laws (Tawḍīḥ al-Masāʾil Jāmiʿ)* in which Āyatullāh al-Sīstānī states:

Issue 310: For a person to perform *wuḍū* with the intention of seeking closeness and sincerity, it is sufficient that one performs it with the intention of obeying the commands of Allah ﷻ; and if one does so with the intention of showing off (to others), or performs *wuḍū* to cool down on a hot day, or anything similar, then that *wuḍū* is invalid.

Issue 311: It is not necessary for a person to say the intention of the *wuḍū* verbally, or even make it pass through one's spiritual heart. Rather, if all the actions of *wuḍū* are performed with the intention of obeying the commands of Allah ﷻ, then that is sufficient.

to be specific to *i'tikāf* - rather, it can be any form of fasting - even if a person is fasting due to having been hired to fast for a deceased individual (it is okay); or it can also be a fast which a person keeps as a recommended fast *(mustaḥabb);* or a lapsed *(qaḍā)* fast.

It is worth mentioning that during the period of fasting, anything that invalidates the fast[114] will also invalidate the *i'tikāf.*

Sixth and Seventh Condition

6. *I'tikāf* must be performed in one of the specific masājid noted below.

Issue 7: *I'tikāf* can only take place in one of the four following masājid:

---

[114] The things which invalidate a fast are:

1. Eating and drinking.
2. Sexual intercourse.
3. Masturbation, meaning that a man - either himself or by means of some object - does something that results in the ejaculation of semen from him.
4. Ascribing false statements to Allah ﷻ, Prophet Muḥammad ﷺ, and his successors [i.e., the Twelve Imams ﷺ], based on obligatory precaution.
5. Causing thick dust to reach one's throat, based on obligatory precaution.
6. Remaining in a state of ritual impurity *(janābah),* menstruation *(ḥayḍ),* or lochia *(nifās).*
7. Applying liquid enema.
8. Vomiting intentionally.

- Masjid al-Ḥarām in Mecca, Arabia
- Masjid al-Nabī ﷺ in Medina, Arabia
- Masjid Kūfa in Kūfa, Iraq
- Masjid Baṣra in Baṣra, Iraq

7. In addition, *iʿtikāf* in the grand/central masjid of any city is also valid.

The only time that this rule [of having *iʿtikāf* in the grand/central masjid of a city] is invalidated is when the prayer leader *(imām)* of that masjid is religiously-deemed to be an unjust person. At that time, based on obligatory precaution, it is not valid to engage in *iʿtikāf* in that particular masjid.

The meaning of the grand/central masjid *(Masjid al-Jāmiʿ)* is a masjid that is not assigned to a particular neighbourhood or region, or that is for a specific group of people. Rather, it is a meeting place for all Muslims from different areas, backgrounds, and neighbourhoods of that city.

It is worth noting that the legitimacy of *iʿtikāf* in other masājid - other than those mentioned above - is not confirmed [by the legal rulings of Islam], however there is nothing wrong with engaging in *iʿtikāf* in those places with the hopes that it will be accepted by Allah ﷻ. However, in a place where there is no proper masjid, engaging in *iʿtikāf* in a building, such as a Ḥusayniyyah, is **not** permitted. Therefore, it must **not** be performed - even if the intention is that one hopes for the rewards and proximity to Allah ﷻ [by engaging in *iʿtikāf* in such a place].

Issue 8: *Iʿtikāf* must be done in ONE masjid. Therefore, *iʿtikāf* cannot be performed in two different masājid, whether they are separate from one another or connected to each other, unless they are connected in such a way that the masses consider those two masājid as being one large masjid.

Issue 9: If the *muʿtakif* sits on a usurped carpet in the masjid and is aware that the carpet is usurped, then they have committed a sin, but their *iʿtikāf* will not be invalidated.

In addition, if a person is sitting in a place in the masjid engaged in *iʿtikāf*, and someone else takes their place in that spot and the former individual who was previously sitting there is not happy with this [losing one's spot], then that second person is considered a sinner, however their *iʿtikāf* will still be correct.

Eighth Condition

8. *Iʿtikāf* must be performed with the permission of someone whose approval is acceptable [and required] in the Islamic legal system *(sharīʿah)*.

Issue 10: *Iʿtikāf* must be with the permission of someone whose permission is binding [and required] under the Islamic legal system *(sharīʿah)*. Therefore, in cases where a person's staying in a masjid is forbidden without the permission or consent of another person, their *iʿtikāf* will be invalid.

By way of a practical example, if performing *iʿtikāf* will cause grief to one's parents, and this distress is due to their compassion for their child; or if a wife leaves the house to engage in *iʿtikāf* without her husband's permission, then such an *iʿtikāf* will be invalid [as in both scenarios the person in question requires the express permission of, in the first case, the parents; and in the second case, the husband].[115]

Ninth Condition

9. The *muʿtakif* must stay in the place of *iʿtikāf* and not leave it, except in cases when leaving - from the point of view of the Islamic legal code *(sharīʿah)* - is permissible [and/or required].

Issue 11: During the period of *iʿtikāf*, an individual must stay in the masjid and cannot leave it except for essential matters; and if they do leave for essential matters, which will be mentioned in the following ruling, then they must not remain outside of the masjid for more than the time that is required to complete the necessary task.

Issue 12: The cases for which leaving the place of *iʿtikāf* is permissible - and in some cases will even become obligatory - are as follows:

a. Necessities which a person has no choice but to leave the masjid for, such as going to the bathroom to relieve oneself.

---

[115] The woman's stay in the masjid [for *iʿtikāf*] is permissible, however if her *iʿtikāf* will take away her husband's [conjugal] rights, then the correctness of her *iʿtikāf* without her husband's permission is problematic [thus, in such a scenario, she must not engage in *iʿtikāf*].

b. Performing the *ghusl* of *janābah.*[116]
c. Performing the *ghusl* of *istiḥāḍā.*[117]
d. Performing *wuḍū* (ablution) for the obligatory *ṣalāt,*[118] or performing an obligatory *ghusl* other than because one is in the state of *janābah,* if performing the *ghusl* or *wuḍū* is not possible inside the masjid,[119] or it is just entirely not possible to perform the *ghusl* or *wuḍū* in

---

[116] In cases where not performing the *ghusl* would cause the individual to remain in the masjid in a state of impurity, or cause the masjid to become impure, then in this case, it is obligatory *(wājib)* to leave the masjid.

[117] If a woman who is in the state of *istiḥāḍā* does not perform her obligatory *ghusl,* then her *i'tikāf* will not be invalidated.

[118] Going out of the masjid to perform *wuḍū* for an obligatory lapsed *(qaḍā)* prayer, if there is sufficient time to make up the prayer (later on), is problematic [and thus must be avoided].

Note from the Translator: The meaning of this ruling is that if a person invalidated their *wuḍū* and they would like to leave the masjid area to perform *wuḍū* so that they can pray an obligatory lapsed prayer that was missed days, weeks, months, or years ago which can be made up at 'any time,' then in this case, they are not permitted to do so. Although a person is advised to make up any lapsed prayers as soon as they can, however when it comes to the rulings of *i'tikāf,* a person is not permitted to leave the masjid to make *wuḍū* to pray a lapsed prayer which can be done at another time.

[119] For example, it will make the masjid impure.

the masjid.[120] and [121]

e. Accompanying a funeral.
f. Preparing the deceased for burial *(ghusl, kafan, hunūt,* etc.).
g. Visiting the sick.
h. *Ṣalāt al-Jumuʿah.*[122]
i. Anything that is considered a customary necessity by the masses.[123]

---

[120] If there is no obstacle to perform the *ghusl* in the masjid and it is possible, then one must not leave the masjid, according to obligatory precaution.

[121] Keep in mind that in some parts of the world, masājid are not like they are in Europe or North America - in that they may not all have roofed structures with carpeting, etc. Some countries may have traditional masājid in which they are open-aired and would have areas for *wuḍū* and possibly an area to perform a *ghusl* - and that entire area would be deemed as a masjid. (Tr.)

[122] It is not permissible for the *muʿtakif* to participate in the congregational prayer *(Ṣalāt al-Jamāʿat)* [the reason why *Ṣalāt al-Jamāʿat* is mentioned here is that *Ṣalāt al-Jumuʿah* can only be performed in congregation, and as such, it goes to reason that if a person wants to perform the Friday prayers, it must be performed in congregation] if it is held outside of the place of *iʿtikāf*, according to obligatory precaution, except for someone who is engaged in *iʿtikāf* in Mecca (inside Masjid al-Ḥarām), as this individual can leave the masjid for congregational or individual prayer and pray anywhere in the city of Mecca.

[123] If for example, it is a customary necessity to participate in examinations in the Islamic Seminary, University, or primary/secondary school exams, then the *muʿtakif* can leave the place of *iʿtikāf* by complying with all other exit conditions.

In all other cases, to leave the masjid for something that is good to do but not a necessity, such as a recommended *wuḍū* or *ghusl*[124] is an area of difficulty, and caution must be observed [thus, one must not leave the masjid for these reasons].

Issue 13: It is not permissible for a *muʿtakif* to leave the masjid to bring in the things one needs [for the *iʿtikāf*] if they can assign a person that is not engaged in the *iʿtikāf* to bring those things for them.

Issue 14: If a *muʿtakif* leaves the masjid for one of the reasons mentioned in **Issue 12**, but the duration of the departure is prolonged in such a way that the outward manifestation of the *iʿtikāf* is lost, then that person's *iʿtikāf* will become invalidated, even if their leaving the masjid was due to compulsion, forgetfulness, necessity, or urgency.

Issue 15: If a *muʿtakif* intentionally and voluntarily leaves the place of *iʿtikāf* in other than the permissible cases, then their *iʿtikāf* will be invalidated, even if the duration of the departure is short such that the form of *iʿtikāf* is not lost. The same ruling applies if the departure is due to not knowing the *sharīʿah* ruling (ignorance of the ruling), or if it is due to

---

However, the duration of their departure should not be prolonged in such a way that the appearance of *iʿtikāf* is lost. For example, there is no problem if a person leaves for around two hours on one of the days for an exam, then returns to the masjid to resume the *iʿtikāf*.

[124] Such as the *ghusl* performed on Friday *(Jumuʿah)*. (Tr.)

forgetfulness. However, if the individual leaves under compulsion or due to an emergency, then their *iʿtikāf* will not be invalidated - except in the case mentioned in **Issue 14**.

Issue 16: If it is obligatory for a *muʿtakif* to leave the masjid but they do not leave, then they are regarded as a sinner, however their *iʿtikāf* will not become invalidated. An example of why they would need to leave could be to follow through with the payment of a debt that a creditor has the right to claim, and its payment necessitates that the individual must leave the place of *iʿtikāf*.[125]

Issue 17: In cases where it is permissible to leave the masjid, the *muʿtakif* must not stay outside of the masjid more than necessary; and when they are outside of the masjid, if possible, they must not sit in the shade during the daytime.[126]

However, if doing the work which is needed to be done cannot be accomplished except by sitting under the shade, then there is no problem; and according to obligatory precaution, after doing the work and eliminating the need, one must not sit under the shade, unless there is a necessity.

---

[125] If a *muʿtakif* enters the state of *janābah*, and intentionally stays in the place of *iʿtikāf* and does not leave the masjid to perform the *ghusl* of *janābah*, then their *iʿtikāf* will become invalidated.

[126] It is worth mentioning that the prohibition of sitting under the shade outside the place of *iʿtikāf* does not relate to the nighttime period, even if it is raining [thus, a person in *iʿtikāf* can go outside and sit under the shade at night when it is raining] - this is in regard to those cases in which it is necessary and permissible for an individual to leave the masjid.

Of course, the *mu'takif* can walk under the shade in cases where it is permissible to leave the masjid, although according to recommended precaution, it is better not to do so.

Issue 18: When leaving the masjid in permissible cases, according to obligatory precaution, it is necessary to choose the shortest route in going and returning to the masjid, unless the choice of a longer route means that the person will be outside of the masjid for a shorter period of time in which case the person should take that path.

Issue 19: A person can make a condition from the beginning, or during the process of making the intention of *i'tikāf* - except in the case of the obligatory *i'tikāf* - that if a problem arises [in their life], they will [break and] leave their *i'tikāf*.

Therefore, by placing this condition, an individual can leave *i'tikāf* - even on the third day - if a particular problem or obstacle arises, and there is nothing wrong with breaking the *i'tikāf* in this way.

However, if the *mu'takif* makes a condition that they will terminate the *i'tikāf* without any reason, then such a condition is not considered valid, based on obligatory precaution.

It is worth noting that placing this condition [the condition of leaving *i'tikāf* during the three days if there is an obstacle] after the start of *i'tikāf* or before it, is not correct. Rather, it should be simultaneous and symmetrical with the intention of *i'tikāf*.

Tenth Condition

10. A person must abandon all the things which are forbidden for a *mu'takif.*

Issue 20: For *i'tikāf* to be correct, it is necessary for a *mu'takif* to avoid the things mentioned below:

1. Smelling a good fragrance (like perfume/cologne).
2. Sexual intercourse.
3. Masturbating, touching, or kissing out of lust - based on obligatory precaution.
4. Arguing.
5. Buying or selling.

It is worth mentioning that doing any of the above things, in addition to being forbidden, also invalidate one's *i'tikāf* according to the Juristic ruling *(fatwā);* and if the *i'tikāf* that was being performed was a definite obligation (such as a person having made a *nadhr* or *qasam* to perform *i'tikāf),* then it must be repeated at a later time.

If the *i'tikāf* being performed was not a definite obligation, then in the case of sexual intercourse it is still impermissible [to engage in this act] according to the *fatwā*; and in other cases, according to obligatory precaution, it is not permissible [to engage in the above noted invalidators of the *i'tikāf*].

Issue 21: It is not permissible for a *mu'takif* to smell any fragrances [perfumes, cologne, etc.] - whether they enjoy smelling it or not; and it is not permissible to smell fragrant plants whether or not they enjoy smelling it; however, there is no problem to smell fragrant plants if they do not enjoy smelling it. A *muʿtakif* can use scented detergents such as liquid or solid soap, shampoo, scented toothpaste, etc.

However, it is not permissible to smell the fragrances that people who are not engaged in *iʿtikāf* usually apply [before coming to pray] in the masjid. But apparently, there is no obstacle in simply 'smelling' the perfume, and it is not necessary to hold (or close) one's nose.

Issue 22: Arguing over worldly or religious issues during *iʿtikāf* is forbidden *(ḥarām)* if it is done with the intention of defeating the other party and asserting one's own [intellectual or personal] virtue and superiority. However, if it is for the purpose of asserting and clarifying the truth, or correcting a mistake of the other party, then it is not impermissible. Therefore, the criterion is the intention of the individual engaged in *iʿtikāf*.

Issue 23: During *iʿtikāf*, buying and selling, and according to obligatory precaution, any type of transaction, such as: Renting something, *muḍārabah*,[127] *muʿāwiḍhah*,[128] or other types of transactions are forbidden *(ḥarām)*, although the actual transaction conducted is valid.

However, if a *muʿtakif* is forced to buy and sell for the preparation of food, or other necessities required for the

---

[127] The term *muḍārabah* refers to a partnership in profit whereby one party provides the capital, and the other party provides the skill and labour.

[128] The term *muʿāwiḍhah* refers to a transaction which involves exchange or bartering of goods or services.

iʿtikāf and has no other way to obtain such necessities,[129] then there is no problem in engaging in such transactions.

Issue 24: If a *muʿtakif* intentionally performs any of the things which are not permissible *(ḥarām)* for one who is in *iʿtikāf* despite knowing the *sharīʿah* ruling; or if they commit it due to ignorance of the issue, however they were not excused in their ignorance [meaning that they had the ability to gain the knowledge on these issues, but willfully or intentionally did not go forth to seek knowledge], then their *iʿtikāf* will be invalid.

However, if they engage in such actions due to forgetfulness or by mistake, or if a person commits one of the actions which invalidates their *iʿtikāf* due to not knowing the issue or was ignorant and unable to get the knowledge, then their *iʿtikāf* will be correct and valid.

---

[129] This means that if a *muʿtakif* does not find another person who is not engaged in *iʿtikāf* to engage in such business transactions on their behalf, and it is not possible to obtain those goods without buying them - such as being gifted or borrowing them - then they are permitted to engage in such transactions.

Rulings of a Lapsed Iʿtikāf

Issue 25: If a *muʿtakif* invalidates their *iʿtikāf* by performing one of the actions which nullifies their *iʿtikāf* mentioned in the previous rulings, and if their *iʿtikāf* was a specified obligatory *iʿtikāf* (due to an oath or promise made to Allah ﷻ), then according to obligatory precaution, they must perform a lapsed *(qaḍā) iʿtikāf*.

However, if it was a non-specified *iʿtikāf*, such as an *iʿtikāf* which was being performed through a vow, but without having specified which time they would perform it, then it is obligatory to re-do that *iʿtikāf* at another time.

Moreover, if it is a recommended *iʿtikāf* and after the end of the second day, a person cancels their *iʿtikāf*, then they must perform the *iʿtikāf* again, according to obligatory precaution.

It is worth mentioning that according to the explanation of **Issue 19**, if a person's *iʿtikāf* was deemed conditional (based on their intention), then even by performing anything which would invalidate the *iʿtikāf*, it is not necessary to resume it or perform its lapse.

Issue 26: If a woman who is in *iʿtikāf* gets her monthly period at any time, then she must leave the masjid immediately. If this happens after the end of the second day of *iʿtikāf*, then the lapse *(qaḍā)* of that *iʿtikāf* will be necessary for her to make up based on obligatory precaution, unless her *iʿtikāf* was conditional, based on what was mentioned in **Issue 19.**[130]

Issue 27: If a person has to perform the lapse of *iʿtikāf*, then it is obligatory to do so, however, it is not an immediate obligation. Nevertheless, one must not delay its performance to such an extent that they are considered as being negligent in fulfilling the obligation; therefore, according to recommended precaution, a person should do one's best to make up the lapse as soon as possible.

Issue 28: If a *muʿtakif* dies during *iʿtikāf*, which was made obligatory by a vow *(nadhr)*, oath *(qasam)*, or promise *(ʿahd)* after the completion of the first two days of *iʿtikāf*, then it is not obligatory for their guardian/*walī* [the eldest son, for example] to perform *iʿtikāf* on their behalf, although based on recommended precaution, the guardian should perform

---

[130] It is worth mentioning that if a woman knows from the beginning that she will menstruate during the three days of *iʿtikāf*, then she must not begin the process of *iʿtikāf*; and if she does still enter the state of *iʿtikāf*, then it will be invalid. In such a scenario, even if she begins her menstruation on the third day of the *iʿtikāf*, then it is not required for her to perform the lapse of it.

i'tikāf on behalf of the deceased.[131]

[131] If a *mu'takif* made a note in one's will that their guardian *(walī)* must perform the *i'tikāf* on their behalf [that they were not able to complete due to their death], then this must be acted upon.

Penalty for Intentionally Invalidating One's I'tikāf

Issue 29: If a *mu'takif* intentionally voids one's obligatory *i'tikāf* by sexual intercourse - whether it is during the day or at night - then an expiation *(kaffārah)* will become obligatory upon them.

With all the other things that break one's *i'tikāf*,[132] there is no expiation/penalty, although according to recommended precaution, it is still advisable to pay it (the penalty).

Issue 30: To fulfill the expiation of voiding one's *i'tikāf* as mentioned in the previous issue, a person must:

1. Free a slave.
2. OR fast for two months - according to what is mentioned in **Issues 1,118 to 1,121**.[133]

---

[132] In the rules of expiation of fasting, if a *mu'takif* does something intentionally during the daylight hours which invalidates the fast, then the expiation of fasting must be performed. The details of this ruling can be found in the book of Islamic Laws under the Chapter of Fasting and the sub-topic of Fasting Expiations.

[133] These rulings are as follows:

Issue 1,118: In cases where a person is required to fast for two consecutive months as an expiation, it is sufficient to fast one full month and one day (a full lunar month, plus one day from the second month) - fasting this entire time [without a break]. In this scenario, if a person does not fast the rest of the days consecutively due to a customary excuse, then there is no problem.

However, if a person does not have a customary excuse, then one must fast the rest of the second month consecutively based on obligatory precaution.

Issue 1,119: With respect to a person who has been obliged to fast for two consecutive months as an expiation, if they start fasting from the first day of a lunar month, then it is sufficient to fast for two full lunar months, even if each of the two months is 29 days.

Of course, a person can start the expiation fasts during the lunar month [rather than starting on the first of the month], but if there is a gap between the fasts of two months such that the continuity of the fasts does not cease to exist according to *sharī'ah* [Details of this ruling are mentioned in **Issue 1,121**], then they must fast for sixty days [In this case, it is necessary to fast thirty-one consecutive days]. If between the fasts, a person does not leave a gap within the two months and does all of them one after the other, then according to obligatory precaution, they must fast for sixty days.

Issue 1,120: A person who is required to fast for two months as an atonement *(kaffārah)* must not start fasting when they know that between the one month and one day that they are required to continuously fast, a day like *'Eid al-Aḍḥā* - on which fasting is forbidden - or the month of Ramaḍān - in which fasting is obligatory - will occur.

This ruling also applies to the atonement for breaking an oath *(qasam)* and the like, where a person must fast for three consecutive days.

Of course, if the fasting is absolute such that it coincides with the fast of the expiation, such as if before the requirement to keep the fast of the expiation, a person vowed to fast on the first day of the month of Rajab, then such fasting which may occur in the course of fasting to cover the expiation will not harm the requirement and acceptability of the fast, and with the intention of the fast of the expiation, it will be accepted [in other words, in such a scenario, a person would be able to 'combine' one's fasting such that the fasting for the expiation is performed, and at the same time they had made a vow to fast on the first day of the month of Rajab, and that vow will also be fulfilled].

However, if a person vowed (kept a *nadhr*) to fast on the first day of the month of Rajab simply out of gratitude for the blessings that Almighty Allah ﷻ has given them, then this will impact the succession of the fasts of the expiation [thus in such a scenario, they would not be permitted to 'combine' these two fasts - unlike what was mentioned in the previous example].

Issue 1,121: If a person does not fast for one or more days during the fasts of the expiation which are required to be carried out consecutively without a valid excuse, then the fasts one performed will not be considered as being a part of the expiation that was obligatory to perform, and that person must repeat the expiation fasts all over again from the beginning.

However, if not being able to fast is due to a valid excuse such as an emergency, illness, necessary travel, or due to menstruation and childbirth - which obviously are out of the control of a woman - then the sequence and continuity of the fasts are not broken in

3. Feed sixty poor people or give each of the sixty poor people one *mudd* of food - which is approximately 750 grams. A person must give the actual food [in kind and not in cash - unless the person is given the cash and expressly directed to spend the money on food stuff and can be trusted to do so]. Some examples of what food items should be given are: wheat, barley, bread, rice, and the like.

If an individual cannot do any of these three mentioned things above, then they need to follow the ruling given in **Issue 1,126.**[134]

---

such instances, however the rest of the fasts must be performed immediately after the situation is resolved.

NOTE: It is worth mentioning that in the above scenario, it is not necessary for a woman to prevent the natural process of menstrual bleeding by taking medication. However, if a woman deliberately causes her period to begin - by taking medication or something else [knowing that her menstrual cycle will begin] - and the succession of expiation fasts will be interrupted, then she must start them all over again.

This ruling is also valid in those cases in which a person does not fast on some days due to forgetting about the expiation they need to offer, or that they make the intention for another fast [other than that of the expiation they are obligated to offer].

[134] **Issue 1,126:** If a person is unable to perform the expiation/penalty of a pledge *(ʿahd)* or the *iʿtikāf*, then one must fast for eighteen days, and it is advisable that these eighteen days are done consecutively - one after the other; and if a person is not even able to complete eighteen days of fasting, then they must [sincerely] ask Allah ﷻ for forgiveness.

Changing Intention from One Form of I'tikāf to Another

Issue 31: It is not permissible to switch from one *iʿtikāf* to another *iʿtikāf* [meaning to change the intention behind why one is performing the *iʿtikāf*, as will be seen in the below examples] even if both are obligatory, such as:

1. A person who made both a vow *(nadhr)* and an oath *(qasam)* - and both were either obligatory or recommended.
2. One of the *iʿtikāf* was obligatory, while the other was recommended.
3. One was for the person themself, while the other was being done on behalf of someone else - either by way of being done on behalf of someone (like one's deceased father), or one was hired to perform it for another person.
4. Both were on behalf of someone else.

This concludes the book, *I'tikāf: The Spiritual Retreat - The Philosophy, Spiritual Mysteries, and Practical Rulings.*

We ask Allah ﷻ to accept our efforts in publishing this book and making it available to the communities to benefit from this magnificent act of worship.

Other Publications Available[1]

1. *A Land Most Goodly: The Story of Yemen in the Quran and in the Times of Prophet Muḥammad and Imam ʿAlī ibn Abī Ṭālib,* by Jaffer Ladak
2. *A Star Amongst the Stars: The Life and Times of the Great Companion: Jabir ibn Abdullah al-Ansari,* by Jaffer Ladak*
3. *Alif, Baa, Taa of Kerbala,* by Saleem Bhimji and Arifa Hudda
4. *Arbāʿīn of Imam Ḥusayn,* compiled and translated by Saleem Bhimji

---

[1] The following is a list of all of the original writings and translations from the Islamic Publishing House. As many of these titles are out of stock, we are slowly re-releasing all of our works via Print-on-Demand through Amazon. Titles with an * after the name are currently available via Amazon from their international platforms, including Australia, Canada, France, Germany, Italy, Japan, UK, USA, Netherlands, and Spain.

If you cannot find any of the above titles on Amazon, feel free to email us at **iph@iph.ca**.

5. *Daily Devotions*, compiled and translated by Saleem Bhimji*
6. *Deficient? A Review of Sermon 80 from Nahj al-Balāgha*, by Āyatullāh al-ʿUẓmā Shaykh Nāṣir Makārim Shīrāzī and translated by Saleem Bhimji
7. *Exegesis of the 29th Juz of the Quran - a Translation of Tafsīr Namuneh*, by Āyatullāh al-ʿUẓmā Shaykh Nāṣir Makārim Shīrāzī and translated by Saleem Bhimji*
8. *Foundations of Islamic Unity* - a translation of *Al-Fuṣūl al-Muhimmah fī Taʾlīf al-Ummah*, by ʿAbd al-Ḥusayn Sharaf al-Dīn al-Mūsawī al-ʿĀmilī and translated by Batool Ispahany*
9. *Fountain of Paradise - Fāṭima az-Zahrāʾ in the Noble Quran*, by Āyatullāh al-ʿUẓmā Shaykh Nāṣir Makārim Shīrāzī, compiled and translated by Saleem Bhimji*
10. *God and god of Science*, by Syed Hasan Raza Jafri*
11. *House of Sorrows*, by Shaykh ʿAbbās al-Qummī and translated by Aejaz Ali Turab Husayn Husayni*
12. *Inspirational Insights*, by Mohammed Khaku
13. *Islam and Religious Pluralism*, by Āyatullāh Shaykh Murtaḍā Muṭahharī and translated by Sayyid Sulayman Ali Hasan
14. *Journey to Eternity - A Handbook of Supplications for the*

Soul, compiled and translated by Saleem Bhimji and Arifa Hudda*

15. *Love and Hate for Allah's Sake,* by Mujtaba Saburi translated by Saleem Bhimji*

16. *Love for the Family,* compiled and translated by Yasin T. Al-Jibouri, Saleem Bhimji, and others

17. *Moral Management,* by Abbas Rahimi and translated by Saleem Bhimji*

18. *Morals of the Masumeen,* by Arifa Hudda

19. *Prayers of the Final Prophet - A Collection of Supplications of Prophet Muḥammad,* by ʿAllāmah Sayyid Muḥammad Ḥusayn Ṭabāʾṭabāʾī and translated by Tahir Ridha-Jaffer*

20. *Prospering Through a Cost of Living Crisis,* by Jaffer Ladak*

21. *Ramaḍān Reflections,* compiled by A Group of Muslim Scholars and translated by Saleem Bhimji*

22. *Ṣalāt al-Āyāt,* by Saleem Bhimji

23. *Ṣalāt al-Ghufaylah: Salvation through Patience & Perseverance,* written by Saleem Bhimji*

24. *Secrets of the Ḥajj,* by Āyatullāh al-ʿUẓmā Shaykh Ḥusayn Mazāherī and translated by Saleem Bhimji

25. *Sunan an-Nabī,* by ʿAllāmah Sayyid Muḥammad Ḥusayn Ṭabāʾṭabāʾī and translated by Tahir Ridha-Jaffer

26. *Tears from Heaven's Flowers: An Anthology of English*

Poetry about the Ahlulbayt, by Abrahim al-Zubeidi

27. *The Day the Germs Caused Fitnah* by Umm Maryam*

28. *The Firmest Armament: Commentary on Āyatul Kursī (The Verse of the Throne),* by Sayyid Nasrullah Burujerdi and translated by Saleem Bhimji*

29. *The Last Luminary and Ways to Delve into the Light,* by Sayyid Muḥammad Ridha Husayni Mutlaq and translated by Saleem Bhimji*

30. *The Muslim Legal Will Booklet,* by Saleem Bhimji*

31. *The Pure Life,* by Āyatullāh al-ʿUẓmā as-Sayyid Muḥammad Taqī al-Modarresī and translated by Jaffer Ladak with commentary by Dr. Zainali Panjwani and Jaffer Ladak*

32. *The Third Testimony: Imam ʿAlī in the Adhān,* compiled and translated by Saleem Bhimji*

33. *The Tragedy of Kerbalāʾ,* as narrated by Imam ʿAlī ibn al-Husayn al-Sajjād 🙏, recorded by Shaykh al-Sadūq and translated by ʿAbdul Zahrāʾ ʿAbdul Ḥusayn*

34. *The Torch of Perpetual Guidance - A Brief Commentary on Ziyārat al-ʿĀshūrāʾ,* by ʿAbbās Azizi and translated by Saleem Bhimji

35. *Weapon of the Believer,* by ʿAllāmah Muḥammad Bāqir Majlisī and translated by Saleem Bhimji*

Upcoming Publications

1. *Shadows of Dissent*, by Āyatullāh Shaykh Nāṣir Makārim Shīrāzī, translated by Saleem Bhimji and the Translation Team of the Islamic Publishing House
2. *Ṣalāt al-Jumuʿah - History, Philosophy, 40 Ahadith on the Importance of Various Ṣalāt, and Practical Rulings*, according to the rulings of Āyatullāh Sayyid ʿAlī al-Ḥusaynī al-Sīstānī, translated by Saleem Bhimji
3. *Knocking on Heaven's Doors*, compiled with translations by Saleem Bhimji
4. *Ramaḍān Devotions - A Collection of Supplications for the Nights of Qadr*, compiled with translations by Saleem Bhimji
5. *Khums: The Fiscal Blueprint for Community Self-Sufficiency*, by Saleem Bhimji
6. *The Comprehensive Book of Marriage and Divorce Formulas*, by Saleem Bhimji
7. *Sex and Spirituality in Islam*, by ʿAlī Ḥusseinzādeh, translated by Saleem Bhimji
8. *Supplication for the People of the Frontiers*, by Shaykh Ḥusayn Anṣāriyān, translated by Saleem Bhimji
9. *The Arbaʿīn: A look into the Ziyarat of Arbaʿīn*, written by Saleem Bhimji

10. *The Young Muslims Daily Devotions Manuals - Volumes I and II,* compiled and translated by Saleem Bhimji

11. *Victor Not Victim: A Biography of Lady Zaynab binte ʿAlī,* researched and written by Saleem Bhimji

In addition to the above, our *Living The Quran Through The Living Quran* series of commentary on the Noble Quran is also being published. To date, we have released the commentary of:

1. Sūrah al-Najm (53)
2. Sūrah Qāf (50)

The commentary of the following chapters of the Quran will also be released in the future:

1. Sūrah al-Fātiḥa (1)
2. Sūrah Yāsīn (36)
3. Sūrah al-Wāqiʿah (56)
4. Sūrah al-Mujādilah (58)
5. Sūrah al-Ṣaff (61)

If you would like to donate to any of our ongoing projects, whether the books, videos, or other publications, you can contribute in the following ways:

1. **Within Canada:** Send an e-transfer from your Canadian bank account to **iph@iph.ca**
2. **International:** Send your transfer via PayPal to **saleem1176@rogers.com**

For more information, contact us at **iph@iph.ca**

اللهم صل على محمد وآل محمد
وعجل فرجهم

Personal Spiritual Development Plan

How to use this Personal Spiritual Development Plan.

Before you fill in the Personal Spiritual Development Plan provided, you should follow the below steps:

1. Take some time to review the below criteria and understand them.
2. Engage in deep, internal introspection as to your personal life and current connection with Allāh ﷻ, Prophet Muḥammad ﷺ and his Ahlul Bayt ؑ, and where you would ideally like to be, spiritually-speaking.

You must realize that for every goal you set for yourself to get back on track spiritually, or to help you continue on your spiritual path and mature, you must reflect upon and implement the below eight pieces of advice to the best of your ability.

Recognize that some goals may take time to achieve - perhaps weeks or months, however, do not ever lose hope or give up - keep continuing to reflect, set goals, and work at them. Most importantly, continue to ask Allāh ﷻ for His help and guidance for you to have the spiritual and physical strength to live up to your fullest potential.

Advice 1: Goal Setting: "Set clear, measurable, and relevant goals with deadlines."

- Objective: Clearly defined and achievable goals.
    - Specify the goal.
    - Measurability (quantifiable outcomes).
    - Relevance to personal growth.

- Time-bound (deadlines).

Advice 2: Self-Assessment: "Reflect honestly on strengths, weaknesses, and opportunities."

- Objective: Honest evaluation of strengths, weaknesses, opportunities, and threats (SWOT analysis).
  - Depth of reflection.
  - Identification of skills/knowledge gaps.
  - Understanding personal values and beliefs.
  - Recognition of external influences.

Advice 3: Action Plan: "Develop detailed steps to achieve your goals effectively."

- Objective: Detailed plan outlining steps to achieve goals.
  - Clarity of action steps.
  - Realistic timeline.
  - Allocation of resources (time, money, etc.).
  - Contingency planning for obstacles.

Advice 4: Skill Development: "Acquire and enhance skills relevant to your growth."

- Objective: Acquisition and enhancement of relevant skills.
  - Identification of target skills.
  - Strategies for skill acquisition (courses, workshops, self-study, etc.).
  - Progress tracking.

    - Application of learned skills in real-life situations.

Advice 5: Feedback Mechanism: "Seek and incorporate feedback to refine your plan."

- Objective: Regular evaluation and adjustment based on feedback.
    - Solicitation of feedback from mentors or peers.
    - Openness to criticism, and willingness to adapt.
    - Integration of feedback into the development plan.
    - Frequency of review and reflection.

Advice 6: Personal Well-being: "Prioritize holistic well-being for sustainable growth."

- Objective: Consideration of holistic well-being (physical, mental, emotional).
    - Balance between personal and professional life.
    - Strategies for stress management and self-care.
    - Awareness of personal boundaries and limits.
    - Regular self-assessment of overall satisfaction and fulfillment.

Advice 7: Accountability: "Take responsibility and stay committed to your plan."

- Objective: Taking responsibility for personal growth.
    - Commitment to the plan.
    - Consistency in following through with action steps.
    - Willingness to seek help or support when needed.
    - Ownership of successes and failures.

Advice 8: Reflection and Adaptation: "Regularly review and adjust your plan based on experience."

- Objective: Continuous learning and adjustment based on experience.
    - Regular reflection on progress.
    - Identification of lessons learned.
    - Adaptation of goals and strategies as necessary.
    - Flexibility in response to changing circumstances.

1. Personal Information:

Name: ______________________________

Date [Gregorian and/or Islamic]: ______________________________

2. Self-Assessment:

i. Spiritual Strengths: List your strengths and what you excel in - such as punctuality in ṣalāt, etc.

____

____

____

____

____

____

____

____

____

____

____

ii. Weaknesses: Identify areas where you need to improve on - such as not wearing *ḥijāb* properly, or not respecting your parents, etc.

iii. Opportunities: Opportunities for spiritual growth, advancement, or learning - such as taking online classes, etc.

iv. Threats: External factors that may hinder your development - such as addiction to social media, etc.

3. Goals:

i. Long-term Goals: Describe your ultimate spiritual objectives and/or aspirations.

ii. Short-term Goals: Break down your long-term goals into smaller, achievable steps.

Goal 1: Specific goal statement

____

____

Measurable outcomes

____

____

Deadline

____

____

Goal 2: Specific goal statement

____

____

Measurable outcomes

____

____

Deadline

____

____

Goal 3: Specific goal statement

Measurable outcomes

Deadline

---

4. Action Plan/Timeline/Measuring Success/Evaluation:

Steps to Achieve Goal 1: List actionable steps for this short-term goal.

Timeline: Outline a timeline for accomplishing this goal and its associated action steps.

Measurement: Define how you will measure progress and success for this goal.

____

____

____

Evaluation: Set dates for evaluating progress and adjusting the plan as necessary.

____

____

____

Steps to Achieve Goal 2: List actionable steps for this short-term goal.

____

____

____

Timeline: Outline a timeline for accomplishing this goal and its associated action steps.

____

____

____

Measurement: Define how you will measure progress and success for this goal.

____

____

____

Evaluation: Set dates for evaluating progress and adjusting the plan as necessary.

____

____

____

Steps to Achieve Goal 3: List actionable steps for this short-term goal.

____

____

____

Timeline: Outline a timeline for accomplishing this goal and its associated action steps.

____

____

____

Measurement: Define how you will measure progress and success for this goal.

____

____

____

Evaluation: Set dates for evaluating progress and adjusting the plan as necessary.

____

____

____

Identify resources required to achieve your goals:

____

____

____

5. Support System: Mentors/Coaches - List individuals who can provide guidance and support to you.

____

____

____

Accountability Partners: Identify someone to hold you accountable for your progress.

____

____

____

6. Reflection: Schedule times for reflecting on your progress, setbacks, and lessons learned.

Date: ______________________________________

Reflection: _________________________________

____

____

Date: ______________________________________

Reflection: _________________________________

____

____

Date: ______________________________________

Reflection: _________________________________

____

____

Date: ______________________________

Reflection: ______________________________

____

____

Date: ______________________________

Reflection: ______________________________

____

____

7. **Adjustment and Flexibility**: Acknowledge the need to adapt the plan based on changing circumstances or new insights.

____

____

____

____

8. **Personal Well-being**: Include strategies for maintaining physical, mental, and emotional well-being while pursuing your goals.

____

____

____

____

I hereby commit myself to this Personal Spiritual Development Plan

Signature: ______________________________

Date: ______________________________

www.ingramcontent.com/pod-product-compliance
Lightning Source LLC
Chambersburg PA
CBHW032005040426
42448CB00006B/486
* 9 7 8 1 9 2 7 9 3 0 5 0 2 *